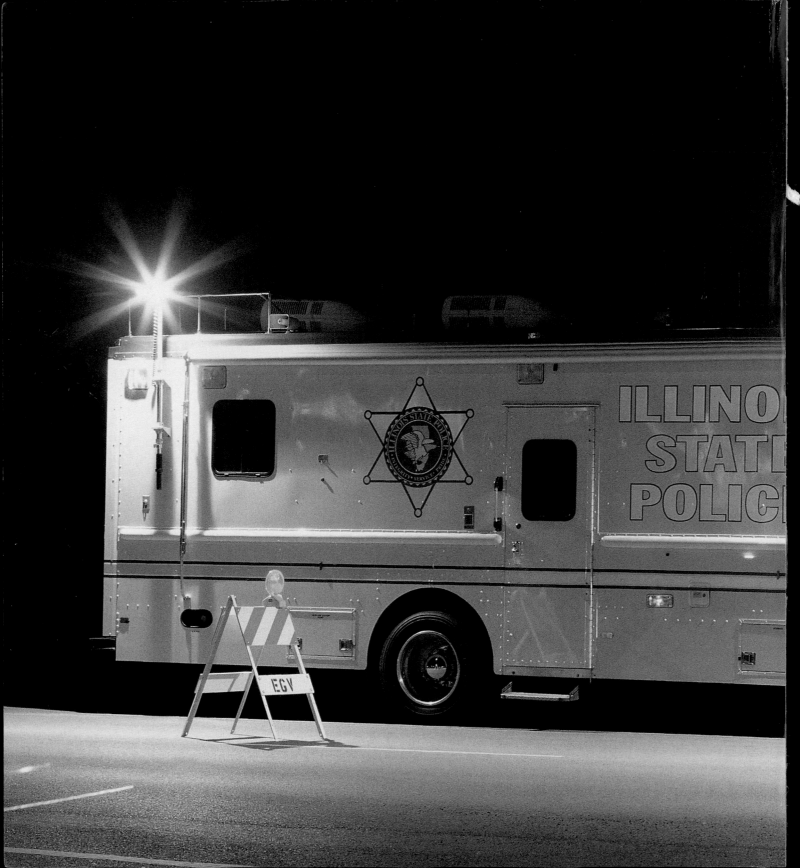

SPECIAL
POLICE
VEHICLES

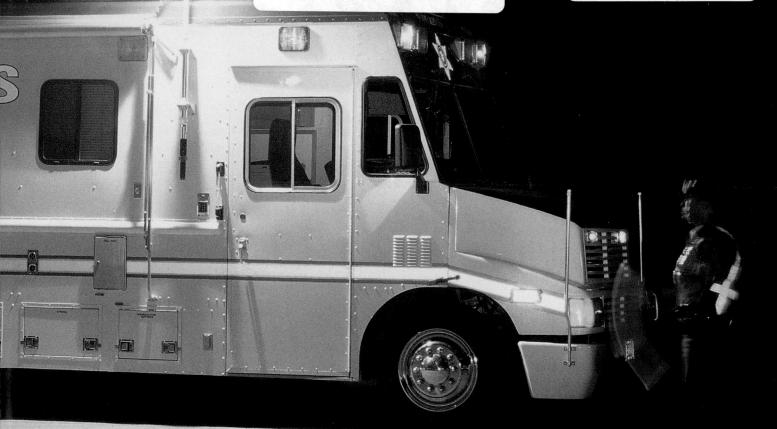

Larry Shapiro

MBI Publishing
Company

First published in 1999 by MBI Publishing Company, 729 Prospect Avenue, PO Box 1, Osceola, WI 54020-0001 USA

MBI Publishing Company books are also available at discounts in bulk quantity for industrial or sales-promotional use. For details write to Special Sales Manager at Motorbooks International Wholesalers & Distributors, 729 Prospect Avenue, PO Box 1, Osceola, WI 54020-0001 USA.

Library of Congress Cataloging-in-Publication Data Available

ISBN 0-7603-0670-2

Printed in China

On the front cover: Oakland County's Dragoon Patroller 2 armored vehicle is the only one of its kind in the Northern Hemisphere. It is capable of 70 miles per hour on land and has the ability to swim in water even when the wheels do not touch the bottom.

On the frontispiece: Livonia is the second largest city in the state of Michigan. Covering 36 square miles, the city has a population of over 110, 000. As recently as 1997, Livonia has been recognized nationally as being one of the safest cities in the country. The SWAT team has two special vehicles at their disposal. The first is this simple bread truck on a Chevy chassis used to transport equipment and personnel. It can also be used as a base for the SWAT commanders. Their second vehicle is depicted on the back cover.

On the title page: The Illinois State Police operates a command and communications vehicle built on an International chassis with a custom interior by LDV. It is shown here working at a roadside safety checkpoint that targets impaired drivers, safety infractions, and other violations.

On the back cover: Livonia, Michigan SWAT also operates this army surplus Peacekeeper armored vehicle. Painted dark blue with "Police" emblazoned in bold letters, the Peacekeeper has a roof gun turret with a shield offering a protected firing position for some scenarios. SWAT's weaponry includes the H&K MP-5, MP-5KPDW, the Colt M-16 and AR-15, Remington 700 and 870 shotguns, Sig Sauer 226, and a 12-gauge Benelli automatic. The team averages four to six full-scale call-outs annually. SWAT utilizes a Special Operations Unit (SOU) within the team as first responders for limited ops that do not require the full 20-member team.

CONTENTS

ACKNOWLEDGMENTS

This book required the help and cooperation of many individuals and organizations. Compiling the information and gaining access to the personnel and vehicles often took quite a bit of scheduling and planning. I would like to thank the individuals who ensured that I had access to the sometimes off-limits areas where some of the teams and vehicles are located.

Thanks to the following people, who are listed alphabetically by department:

Bannockburn, IL, Police Department: Deputy Chief Kevin Tracz, NIPAS-EST Coordinator.

Bureau of Alcohol, Tobacco, and Firearms: Harry Eberhart, Western Team Leader, and Dave DiBetta.

Dearborn, MI, Police Department: Sergeant Gary Muraca, Corporal Mike "Goose" Christoft, and Corporal Todd Hoffman.

Detroit Metropolitan Wayne County Airport: Alfred James, Director of Public Safety, and Kim James.

Livonia, MI, Police Department: Officer Ron Proudlock, SPO and M.T.O.A. President.

Louisville, KY, Police Department: Lieutenant Mike Doosett, Lieutenant Don Durbrink, Sergeant Ozzy Gibson, PIO Officer Aaron Graham, PIO Officer Eric Johnson, Captain Steve Thompson, and Detective Tom Schneider.

Los Angeles County Sheriff's Department: Lieutenant Joe Gutierrez; Deputy Terry Ascherin, Special Enforcement ESD; and Deputy Mike Wilber, Special Enforcement Bureau SED.

Los Angeles Police Department: Lieutenant Greg Roper; Sergeant Paul Walters; Officer Tim Cooper, Officer Dennis Gilbert, and Officer Patricia Guessferd, LAPD Bomb Squad; Officer Ed Waschak and Officer William Young, LAPD Incident Command Post Unit; Detective Supervisors Roosevelt Joseph and Sal LaBarbera, LAPD South Bureau Homicide; Sergeant Clyde Conly, Officer John Kent, Officer Dan Skinner, and Officer Steven Stear, LAPD SWAT.

Lynch Diversified Vehicles: Larry Laguardia.

Miami-Dade Police Department, FL: Sergeant Pete Andreu and Detective Ed Munn, Media Relations; Officer Dan Eydt and Officer Moe Smith, Bomb Squad; Sergeant Peter Caroddo, Officer Troy Lee, and Officer Jorge Herrera, SRT; Officer John Rojas, Northside Station; and Officer Susan Bedal, Community Affairs.

Michigan State Police: Sergeant Warren Miller, Sergeant Joseph Thomas, Sergeant Andrew Wing, and David Verhougstraete.

NYPD: Lieutenant Sean Crowley, DCPI; Lieutenant Chris Ellsion, ESU; Officer David Kayen and Officer Mat McCarthey, ESU Eight-Truck; Officer Richard Bosetti, Officer John Ehlich, Officer Charlie O'Connor, and Officer Mike Lamagna, ESU Floyd Bennet Field Eleven-Truck; Officer Ray Butkiewicz and Officer Jim Hunt, ESU Seven-Truck.

Oakland County Sheriff's Department, MI: Sergeant Dale A. Romeo.

Orange County Sheriff's Office, FL: Commander Matt Weathersby, Lieutenant Emmett Hummel, Sergeant Joe Carter, Sergeant Paul Hopkins, Deputy Todd Gardiner, Deputy First Class Dave Thompson, and Glenn Miller.

Scottsdale, AZ, Police Department: Tracie Fife and Stephen Toubus.

Wayne County, MI, Airport Police: Lieutenant David Quinn; Sergeant Mark Bonza and Sergeant Bill Dunbar, Special Response Unit; Corporal Paul Molitor and Corporal Pete Molitor, Explosive Ordnance Division.

Westchester County Police, NY: Officer Danny Carfi and Officer Dan Langford.

Wyoming Police Department, MI: Officer Jill Bishop, Officer Joe Steffes, and Officer Jeff Whitcomb.

Yonkers, NY, Police Department: Lieutenant Joseph Barca, Officer Jorge Cordero, and Officer Sean Moran, ESU.

My sister Barbara has asked to be acknowledged as both my inspiration and the source of everything I've ever learned. So, to Barbara, I say thank you and now get off my back.

I would have been unable to assemble and finish this book without the support, love, and help of my wife Dorothy, who continues to expand her knowledge into areas in which she never knew she had an interest. When we went to Scottsdale, AZ, to relax, she shocked me by suggesting a visit to the police department for inclusion in this book. She continues to surprise me in different ways and always keeps life interesting.

INTRODUCTION

The services provided by police departments have increased in the past decades to include both public education and public protection. Many departments have had the need to supplement the basic functions of patrol with special divisions, bureaus, and teams that are highly trained to handle other duties.

This book highlights the special deployment vehicles that are used by local, county, state, and city departments. Although much of the focus deals with Special Weapons and Tactics (SWAT) teams, other unique areas of operation are illustrated, including bomb squads and mobile emergency command posts.

There are no big secrets being revealed here to jeopardize the safety or efficiency of these teams. If anything, this book might serve to deter those who take it upon themselves to break the law and come in contact with any of the tactical teams or the skilled bomb technicians portrayed. Although several police agencies wish to have their special deployment vehicles remain hidden and covert, others would like everyone to know their capabilities. Citizens feel more comfortable and secure in knowing the level of professionalism and protection that is being provided to them. The criminal or mischievous element might think twice about crossing paths with the men and women who are providing these services.

CHAPTER ONE

CITY DEPARTMENTS

Dearborn, Michigan

Dearborn is possibly best known as the world headquarters of the Ford Motor Company. The city is just over 25 square miles and the police department has 203 sworn personnel. The fleet for patrol and supplemental vehicles is comprised of Ford Crown Victorias, Explorers, Tauruses, and a Ford chassis under the mobile command van.

An interior view of the Wyoming, Michigan, TACT truck shows the ceiling-mounted grab rails. Team members approach their objective standing so they will have their weapons ready when they go.

A 1958 armored car provides protection for the Dearborn, Michigan, SWAT team in the event that a hostile barricaded subject fires at officers. Fitted with a 10-foot ram at the front, this truck will knock down a door and provide cover for an entry team.

Dearborn has a SWAT team that is made up of 16 members. They work and train with a five-member crisis negotiation team (CNT). Two of the SWAT team members are Emergency Medical Technicians (EMTs), and as of this writing, the team is also working to incorporate fire department medics. The team currently handles an average of 6–7 barricaded subjects a year.

One of the more disturbing trends for this and other SWAT teams is responding to an incident that is referred to as "suicide by cop." This involves a hostile subject who is armed and wants to commit suicide but doesn't have the ability to do it. The individual threatens the police with the use of deadly force in an attempt to draw their fire and be killed. Teams approach situations like this hoping to refrain from deadly force by using "less-lethal" rounds, also referred to as "beanbags." Resembling a small beanbag, these rounds are deployed from a 12-gauge shotgun to knock assailants down without mortally wounding them. The impact of a beanbag round can be compared to being hit by a fastball from a major league pitcher. The intent is to aim for one of the subject's extremities. These rounds are labeled "less-lethal" and not "non-lethal," because there are no guarantees. If an individual is struck square in the chest or head, for instance, the round could prove to be lethal.

When two subjects wearing body armor and carrying automatic rifles terrorized a neighborhood in Los Angeles with firepower that was superior to the patrol division officers', many departments across the country evaluated their own ability to respond to a similar situation. Dearborn, MI, developed the "S" car, a patrol car to be staffed by at least one SWAT officer with various weapons, enabling him or her to engage and mitigate incidents with heavily armed suspects before the full SWAT team can deploy.

The department has two special deployment vehicles, both part of the SWAT team. The first unit is a 1978 Ford 350 Econoline chassis with a simple box-style body. Team members outfitted the interior. The primary functions for this vehicle include transportation of team members, a base for incident commanders, and storage for weapons and small equipment including a portable ram for forcibly opening doors.

The second unit is a 1958 truck, commonly known as an armored car, acquired from an armored car company (which explains why it has a Chevy and not a Ford chassis). This unit provides the team with certain capabilities that a conventional vehicle would not. An entry team can make an approach, then deploy from the side or rear door and walk behind the truck for protection. The roof has a hatch that is ideal for a 37-mm device to deploy gas into a hostile environment. The front is fitted to accommodate a 10-foot ram for breaking through doors. There are three height settings: 2-feet, 6-feet, and 7 1/2-feet for different types of buildings, such as a house with a front porch versus a house with a ground-level entry. In the event that officers would be put at risk using a portable ram, the truck can drive right up to the door and force it in while the team is protected by the truck's armor. Snipers will gather the information necessary to determine the proper position for the ram when it is needed. The armored car can also be used as a distraction

device while the team prepares to make entry from a different direction.

On any given call-out, the main objective for the team is to gather data for the negotiators and a safe entry if needed. With this in mind, the team has a four-tiered approach to tactical situations. The number one preference is for the negotiators to resolve the situation. If that fails, the next hope is to make an entry and convince the subject or subjects that it is in their best interest to surrender to the better-trained and armed force. The next objective would be to end the mission with non-lethal force, and the last would be a successful lethal solution with no injuries to the team members.

Our society often learns from the misfortune of others. This was the case for SWAT teams around the country when two heavily armed individuals in full body armor terrorized a Los Angeles neighborhood with more firepower than was then assigned to the patrol division. As with any SWAT deployment, there was a delay in the time it took for team members to arrive on the scene. The Dearborn Police adapted their protocol in response to the Los Angeles event by adding an additional unit to their SWAT team. Labeled the "S" car, one patrol car has been specially outfitted for team members. Although there are no external markings to differentiate this from other cars, the S car has a SWAT officer on each tour of duty. This ensures the ability to get firepower to a scene rapidly, before the team assembles. Assuming command until the team is assembled, the SWAT officer has a virtual arsenal at his or her disposal, which allows him or her to mitigate some missions early on. In addition to the SWAT officer's individual gear, the car is stocked with several weapons, a medical kit, black smoke grenades, tear gas, stun grenades, less-lethal beanbag rounds, regular shotgun shells, and slugs.

Not knowing just what variables the mission will present, the different shotgun rounds give the officers a choice. In contrast to the beanbag rounds, the shotgun shells and slugs are lethal. Shells consist of "OO," double odd buck shot, which when fired spray small pellets from the gun. The spread of these pellets is about 1 inch per yard, requiring a relatively close proximity to the target. Extremely accurate aim is not a priority here since some of the spray will hit any target that is close enough. In contrast, a slug is a single projectile that travels farther than shells and requires more accuracy. In close quarters, a slug would require more time to fire accurately than shells. Similarly, if the target is a fair distance away, shells would either not reach the target, or the amount of buck shot that hit would not be enough to neutralize the target. One use for the shells is as backup for the beanbag rounds.

Weapons in the S car include an H&K model 93 .223-caliber long-range perimeter rifle, a Colt AR-15 semiautomatic .223-caliber perimeter rifle, and an H&K MP-5 9-mm semi-or fully automatic entry weapon with a lighting system.

Also at the ready is a Remington 870 12-gauge shotgun with a short stock and 14-inch short barrel, as well as a Remington 870 shotgun with a full stock, a full 20-inch barrel, and a light for door breaches. The 9-mm weapon is preferred during entry to the .223-caliber gun. The .223-caliber rounds can penetrate interior walls, endangering officers in other rooms with friendly fire.

Louisville, Kentucky

The city of Louisville has a population of 280,000 people. The police department maintains a force of 672 sworn officers distributed over five districts. The department utilizes a para-military command structure with the highest-ranking chief officer carrying the rank of full colonel. The next level of command consists of three deputy chiefs with the rank of lieutenant colonel. The mayor appoints all of the colonels, and the full colonel has always come from within the department. A major who is appointed by the colonel represents the next level. The rest of the force is made up of civil service personnel with the rank of captain, lieutenant, sergeant, and officer, in decreasing rank.

The Louisville department prefers this structure since it provides a clear-cut rank and chain of command. The department was formed after the Civil War in 1806 and prides itself on progressive ideas and innovation. One example of being ahead of the times was evident in the 1940s when the department installed radios in squad cars instead of using the popular call boxes on street corners. Recently, the department has been implementing community-focused policing based on making duties customer-oriented. They currently boast a moderate crime rate with an average of 68 murders annually.

In addition to patrolling the city proper, the department has responsibility for policing all of the highways that run through the city's

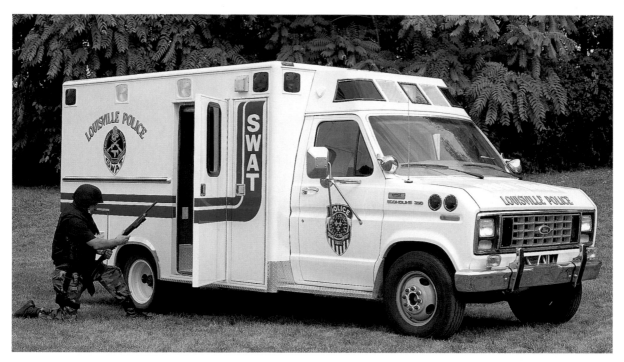

A member of the Louisville SWAT team checks his weapon outside the SWAT truck. Although team members will respond to a call-out in their patrol cars, the truck stores additional equipment and ammunition and provides a place for officers to change into their BDUs.

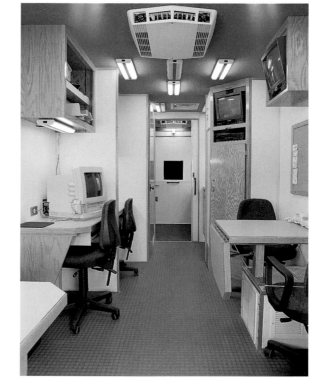

The interior of the HNT shows several workstations, a rear conference room, electronic equipment, and an additional drop-lid worktable. All of the countertops and compartment sides are formica and the cabinetry is custom hardwood.

Although this command unit is primarily for the use of the HNT, anyone in the department can request it to assist with a major incident. Grumman-Ohlsen built the body on a Chevrolet chassis. LDV built the custom interior to the specifications from the Louisville PD.

corporate limits. They utilize Chevy Tahoes and Camaros, all of which are not fully marked. Roughly 300 Ford Crown Victorias, supplemented with bike patrols in every district, handle normal patrol functions. There are several special teams within the department. These include SWAT, the Hostage Negotiating Team (HNT), Rapid Anti-Disturbance (RAD), the Dignitary Protection Team (DPT), the Hazardous Device Unit (HDU), and the Underwater Recovery Team (Scuba) that works with the fire department. SWAT, HNT, and HDU have special deployment vehicles for their teams.

SWAT handles barricaded subjects, high-risk warrant service, and hostage scenarios. The team is comprised of about 28 officers who train together on a regular basis. Averaging 60–65 call-outs annually, team members respond to an incident in their squad cars and one person is assigned the responsibility of bringing the van to the scene. Each member

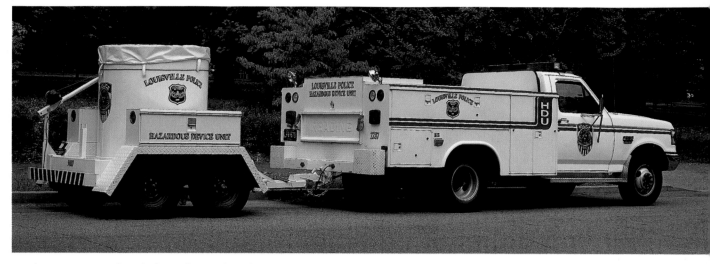

The HDU responds with this utility truck and the top-venting TCV when a live ordnance is discovered. It can withstand a blast on the order of five sticks of dynamite.

carries a gear bag and can use the van for changing into a basic duty uniform (BDU) if desired. The SWAT vehicle is built on a 1984 Ford F350 Econoline chassis with a 460-ci V-8 engine. The body, which resembles an ambulance, was specially designed and built by the Collins Company. It features gun racks, two benches for the transport of team members, storage of tear gas with a six-round drum gas launcher, grenades, distraction devices, battering rams, ladders, cutters, chains, vests, and ballistic shields.

Weaponry that may be carried in the van includes sniper rifles, Uzis, MP-5s, and Mini-14s that are being replaced by AR-15s. Additional armaments include an MP-5 with a scope and silencer for putting out streetlights, a Remington 870 shotgun with less-lethal force beanbag rounds, and a Remington 870 12-gauge with a shot-block assembly to explode door locks while controlling the scrap metal and shrapnel.

The department uses a point system to evaluate the level of risk involved in serving warrants. Based on known factors, various elements of the warrant are given point values. When the summation is completed, a point total of 24 requires the SWAT team to execute the warrant, and a total ranging from 15 to 20 allows the officer in charge to request assistance from SWAT.

The HNT has in the area of 20 members who are divided into two teams. Each team consists of primary and secondary negotiators, and a commander, in addition to support and intelligence-gathering personnel. Their truck has a 1990 Chevrolet chassis with a 225-horsepower V-8 engine, and a 1992 30-foot Grumman-Ohlsen body. The interior was designed and outfitted by Lynch Diversified Vehicles (LDV) and is divided into two separate compartments. The rear compartment has a conference area with privacy for the primary and secondary negotiators. The front section has several workstations and computers for five team members to gather information and communicate with others. The truck is equipped with a bathroom, generator, and convenience items including a refrigerator and microwave oven for prolonged incidents. On the outside of the truck is a retractable awning for an outside command post. Supplemental equipment carried onboard includes 10,000 feet of phone wire for establishing communications with a barricaded subject, cellular communications, a portable phone system, and several television sets with VCRs to record and monitor the local news media. The HNT truck is also used as a mobile command post for non-hostage incidents when deemed necessary by the district commanders.

The HDU, also known as the bomb squad, handles all security sweeps prior to various public events in addition to responding whenever a suspicious device is reported. They will respond to an area within a 250-mile radius of Louisville, including locations in Indiana. Police headquarters receives hundreds of threats annually, though most turn out to be nothing at all. HDU uses a 1989 Ford F350 truck that has a Reading body outfitted with storage compartments. It carries two bomb suits, two pan disrupters to detonate a device by remote control, various tools to collect evidence, laser sights, nonelectric lines for detonation, generators, radiation detectors, two portable x-ray machines, and a complete communications system for the commander and the bomb technicians on-scene. They also have a top-loading total containment vessel (TCV) on a trailer that is pulled by the utility truck. The trailer has a winch to lift a device and place it into the containment vessel. This chamber is considered a single use vessel depending on the severity of the blast that occurs within it. Small pipe bombs and other ordnances with a low blast power will not damage the chamber, but a blast on the order of six sticks of dynamite will affect the vessel's integrity, rendering it useless for further devices.

Scottsdale, Arizona

The city of Scottsdale is located along the northern edge of Phoenix and covers 185.2 square miles. The city's population has grown to 200,000 in recent years and is expected to double in the

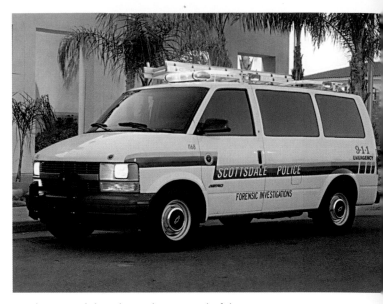

The Scottsdale Police utilize several of these vans, which resemble a local phone company service vehicle. They serve as a base for the gathering of forensic evidence at all crime scenes. The forensic technicians are civilian personnel.

An inside look at the Forensic Investigations van shows storage compartments for tools, evidence containers, and other supplies that are used by the technicians.

This command and communications unit provides the Scottsdale Police Department with a state-of-the-art command center to coordinate large-scale, multi-jurisdictional, or multi-agency incidents. It is also a vital resource for the regional DUI task force that concentrates on keeping drunk drivers off the roads.

next five years. The city itself has literally grown out of the desert into a lush community largely inhabited by people moving south for warmer climates and "snow birds" who descend on the city to escape during the cold winters months.

The Scottsdale Police Department is an internationally accredited department. As of this writing, they have roughly 320 sworn officers who are backed up by a civilian staff of more than 200 personnel. The civilian members handle functions in the city including crime scene and forensics work, equipment and vehicle logistics, community service work, and traffic duties. Differentiated by blue uniforms to the sworn officer's tan, the civilian workers use fully marked police vehicles to perform their duties.

The department is divided into four main bureaus. One is the Uniformed Services Bureau that oversees the Special Operations Division, which has a canine unit with seven dogs, a 12-member bike unit, and a mounted unit. The Investigative Services Bureau has units for personal and property crimes, gang, youth, and crisis intervention, and the Special Investigations Unit, which includes the SWAT team, for assisting with drug seizures, high-risk warrant service, and barricaded subjects.

Scottsdale operates several special vehicles within its fleet including Ford Explorers for the canine and Drug Abuse Resistance Education (D.A.R.E.) units, a pickup truck and trailer for the mounted unit, minivans for the forensic technicians, a Blue Bird bus for command purposes,

17

and nondescript vans for the SWAT team and hostage negotiators.

The crime lab runs five mobile evidence units for technicians' use in performing forensic work at crime scenes. During 1997, they processed almost 2,500 crime scenes. One unit sits as a backup, while the other four are on patrol between the hours of 7 A.M. and 3 A.M. With two units north and two south, these civilian technicians are kept quite busy. In Scottsdale, evidence is collected at every crime scene. The crime lab uses GMC minivans that resemble local cable or phone service repair trucks, with ladder racks on the roof and compartmentation on the inside for the storage of tools and equipment used for the gathering of evidence. The department has strict guidelines for units running "code 3" (using lights and sirens). The evidence units are not emergency vehicles and therefore do not respond code 3. Since the department is accredited and the units have full police markings, it is mandated that they must also have emergency lights and sirens.

The department also has a state-of-the-art mobile command post. The unit is called the Public Safety Command Van (PSCV) and is built on a 35-foot-long 1997 Blue Bird bus chassis that resembles a school bus. A six-cylinder, turbocharged Cummins engine powers the PSCV. The interior was built by the Mattman Company and is divided into three sections.

The front area has several stations with phones, radios, and computers for use as a command post at large incidents or special functions. Each city department has an assigned position with radios to communicate with their vehicles in the event of deployment. One of the exterior entrances is located in the front section. The center section has a lavatory and a galley with a refrigerator, water cooler, and other amenities to enable the occupants to be self-sufficient on-scene. The rear of the unit is prepared for multiple

The rear section of the command unit was designed with a restraint chair to draw blood from DUI suspects during an investigation. The blood is drawn by a phlebotomist and placed in a refrigerator that is used solely for blood storage. This section of the bus has its own exterior door so the suspects only enter this area.

uses. Counters and phones provide additional space for command personnel or for data gathering. This area can also be used to process prisoners, to conduct field interrogations, and to brief officers at a major incident. There is video and audio equipment, a fax and copy machine, and two-way radios.

Beyond these capabilities, however, the principal work that is performed in the rear area relates to ridding the road of drunk or impaired drivers. The command bus is part of a regional Driving Under the Influence (DUI) Task Force. Used extensively during the major holidays, the bus is set up at area roadblocks where officers look for drivers who are DUI. Unlike some cities, this task force does not administer breathalyzer tests to motorists suspected of exceeding the legal blood alcohol level. Drivers are required to submit a blood sample. This is a non-negotiable test. If the driver refuses to voluntarily have blood drawn, the officers will contact a judge and get a warrant, any time of the day or night.

The bus is equipped with a 20-kW diesel generator, an exterior canopy that rolls down to provide protection from the hot sun for officers and command personnel, a telescoping light tower on the roof with four 500-watt halogen lights, and televisions with cameras to record interrogations. The PSCV has a 100-watt radio transmitter/receiver and telephone communications switching equipment that can adapt to land line service and cellular- or satellite-based systems. External compartments contain drink-ing water, cords for a shoreline power hookup, tables and chairs, an additional telephone, and gun cabinet.

Wyoming, Michigan

Located just outside of Grand Rapids, the city of Wyoming is the second largest city in Kent County. It covers 26 square miles and has a nighttime population of 70,000. The police department of 101 sworn officers has a Tactical Arrest and Confrontation Team (TACT) that responds to an average of 20 call-outs annually. The majority of

The Wyoming, Michigan, TACT uses this armored car that was sold to the department when it was retired from service. This unit is a 1960s-vintage truck with a GMC 6000 chassis and a V-6 gasoline engine. The driver's area is separated from the rear section where the crew rides when the unit is placed into service.

these missions involve high-risk search and arrest warrants while the balance deals with barricaded individuals. Currently the part-time team is 15 strong and employs two special vehicles.

The older of the two is an armored car that was sold to the department when it was retired from the service of transporting money. This unit is a 1960s-vintage truck with a GMC 6000 chassis and a V-6 gasoline engine. The driver's area is separated from the rear section where the crew rides in the event the unit is placed into service.

The other unit is the team's brand-new truck for team transport, command, and equipment storage. This unique vehicle is built on a custom chassis that, until 1998, had been used exclusively for fire trucks. The chassis was supplied by HME, Inc., which is located within the city limits

The new tactical truck for the Wyoming, Michigan, TACT is built on a HME fire truck chassis. The large rear body can transport the entire team to a call-out. Here, tactical officers demonstrate how the truck is used when they arrive on-scene. Each member files out the forward-facing door to form their snake line.

of Wyoming. The tilt-cab model is an 1871 SFO and features a 275-horsepower Cummins ISB engine with an Allison automatic transmission. The cab features seating for five with a full bench seat across the back. A walk-through passage was cut into the rear of the cab to gain access to the body of the truck from inside the cab.

The body was built by Cresco out of Iowa, and the interior was designed and built-out by a company that was formed by several of the Wyoming TACT officers. The rear features bench seating with seatbelts for 12 as well as custom storage cabinets and a command post. The bench seating has storage underneath for each officer's gear bag. One of the large interior cabinets is for the storage of guns that include AR-15s, MP-5s, Remington 870 and Benelli entry shotguns, and additional 870s for less-lethal rounds. A twin cabinet stores reload ammunition, smoke and tear gas, and diversionary devices. Additional storage is designated for the two-person sniper teams. Their long guns, binoculars, spotting scopes, night vision gear, and ground mats are stored there. The rearmost portion is the command post with a TV, VCR, fax, phones, and multiple radios. The negotiators will set up shop in the bench area after the team arrives and exits the truck.

External components include a retractable awning, phone jacks for four different lines, AC outlets and cable TV inputs, storage space for a 7-kW generator, tripods, tables and folding chairs, ballistic shields, and entry tools.

The body of the truck was designed to transport the full team to a barricaded subject or hostage incident as well as for deployment when the team executes warrants. Front and side windows in the rear section allow the team to view their objective as they approach. This helps them use the element of surprise by enabling them to plan a swift exit from either side of the unit when they are approximately one house away from the objective. Formerly, they had to exit the vehicle from the rear and only the driver could view the actual house before the team hit the street running. TACT was established 25 years ago and has never had to use lethal force to resolve an incident.

Yonkers, New York

The city of Yonkers, with a population of 187,000, is located in Westchester County, directly north of New York City. Department of Justice statistics for 1997 rated it as one of the safest cities in the United States. Compared to cities with populations over 150,000, Yonkers had the fourth lowest crime rate out of the top 100 cities. The city is divided into four police precincts, with over 559 uniformed personnel. Specialized, nonpatrol responses are handled by the Emergency Services Unit (ESU), which is a detachment within the police department. The ESU works within each precinct under the precinct commander. Additionally, the ESU has its own lieutenant who oversees extended ESU incidents and all tactical jobs. Usually, two ESU officers per precinct are on patrol during each tour with a Chevy Suburban or one of their specially designed response "trucks." The ESU officers have normal patrol functions that are superceded by ESU calls. They have no assigned patrol sector within each precinct and may be called to a job anywhere citywide.

The ESU officers are easily recognizable since they do not wear badges on their shirts and their daily uniform consists of BDUs. Instead, each officer's badge number and name is embroidered on a patch and sewn onto his or her shirt.

Duties assigned to the ESU include all tactical situations, first responder calls for medical emergencies, vehicle accident extrication, animal calls, high angle rescues, surface water rescues, elevator rescues, and motor vehicle accident investigations where injuries occur. Underwater rescues will be handled by another agency as

This is one of Yonkers' new ESU response trucks that is ready to receive police markings and be put into service. It can carry more equipment than the Suburban and insulates the officers from shifting cargo and the gasoline smell from the onboard gas generator.

It may be hard to visualize a Chevy Suburban carrying all of the equipment described for use by the Yonkers ESU. It's a very tight fit but everything has a place and is accessible to go into action.

well as the city of New York Harbor Unit, which can respond quickly with helicopters and divers.

In Yonkers, the ESU takes care of many situations that would initiate a fire department response elsewhere. For example, the police department ESU and not the fire department will handle motor vehicle accidents without fires or dangerous fluid spills. This includes accidents with victim entrapment that require the use of hydraulic rescue tools. Each ESU vehicle has a

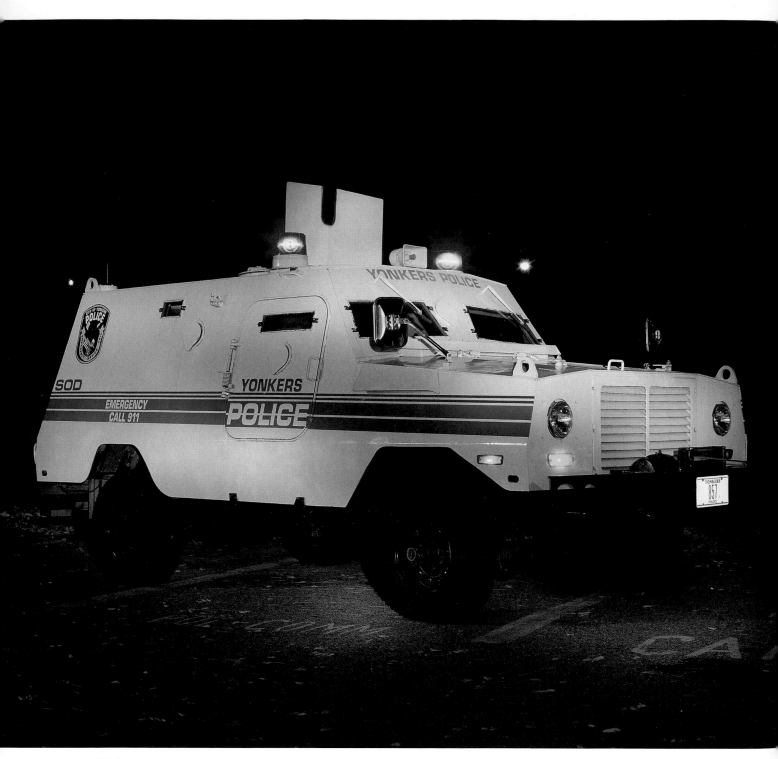

complement of spreaders, rams, and cutters. These calls make up a large part of the duties handled by the ESU on a daily basis.

Medical calls account for the vast majority of ESU responses. Depending on the type of call received by the police 9-1-1 dispatch center, an EMS call can result in an ESU or fire department response. For example, the fire department will handle complaints relating to cardiac problems or breathing difficulty, and pregnancy. The ESU will respond to motor vehicle accidents, falls, home accidents, crimes, and calls of an unknown nature.

Many of the ESU's responses are tactical jobs involving barricaded subjects, hostage scenarios, emotionally disturbed persons (EDPs), and high-risk warrant service. Their patrol vehicles carry each officer's personal gear along with weapons and supplies assigned to the unit. Personal gear consists of a tactical vest, Kevlar helmet and gloves, gas mask, Nomex hood, elbow and knee pads, protective eye gear, and an officer's individual weapon for specialized assignments (a sniper's rifle, for example). Weapons assigned to the vehicles include two MP-5s and several shotguns for breaching and firing less-lethal rounds.

Over 95 percent of ESU officers are EMTs, and some are full paramedics. The ESU vehicles carry basic life support (BLS) equipment, ice-rescue suits, personal flotation devices for surface water rescues, a K-12 saw, cribbing, air cylinders, and a gas generator for the hydraulic tools in addition to the tactical weapons and gear. The Suburbans have four-wheel-drive capabilities and allow for quicker responses as well as having smaller generators than the larger response trucks. The trucks are built on

Chevy pickup chassis and have bodies with several compartments allowing for better organization of the equipment. Trucks carry various items that are not on the Suburbans, including a stokes basket, a ladder, quartz lights, a winch, front bumpers for pushing vehicles, and a truck-mounted generator capable of providing electric power. One advantage of the response truck over the Suburban is the separation of the passenger compartment from the equipment storage. The generators carried on the Suburbans sometimes give off a gas odor, and a sudden stop can cause some supplies to bump the back of the front seat.

Each officer assigned to the ESU undergoes 120 hours of rescue, medical, tactical, and weapons training above the normal training for patrol officers. Jobs requiring additional manpower will receive additional ESU units from the other precincts. In the event of a medivac helicopter landing, ESU handles the landing zone.

Canine officers are cross-trained with ESU, with the exception of the medical training, and will act as supplemental personnel on ESU jobs. They will assist with entry on tactical operations or as added manpower for vehicle extrications.

The Yonkers Police Department maintains a military surplus Peacekeeper armored vehicle for officer safety on tactical jobs where they are being fired upon. This is not a covert unit. It is fully marked to match all of the department vehicles. Yonkers ESU officers also respond to calls for tactical help from other police departments in Westchester County. There they may work with other teams, including the Westchester County team.

Some departments choose to keep their Peacekeeper as a covert vehicle. Yonkers has painted and lettered theirs to match the balance of the police fleet complete with lights and siren.

CHAPTER TWO

LOS ANGELES CITY AND COUNTY

Los Angeles City

The city of Los Angeles has a population in excess of 3.69 million people in an area that encompasses 468 square miles of Southern California. The Los Angeles City Police Department (LAPD) provides protection for this area and employs almost 9,700 sworn officers plus just under 3,000 civilians. The city is divided into four police bureaus: the South, Central, West, and the Valley Bureaus, which are further broken down into 18 geographic divisions.

One of LAPD's two V100 armored vehicles is stationed in a central location to provide the team with protection from sniper fire. Both units were put into service during the Watts riots to rescue officers who were pinned down.

This Los Angeles County ARV is an army surplus Peacekeeper that has permanently mounted skids on the sides. Officers can ride the skids on one side and receive protection from the unit's armor when deploying under fire.

South Bureau Homicide Unit

Each division has a detective unit with juvenile, rape, burglary, and homicide units. In 1989, an experimental unit was established, the South Bureau Homicide Unit, to handle all homicides for the four divisions that compose the South Bureau of the city. These included the 77th Street Division, the Southeast, Southwest, and the Harbor Divisions. These divisions had the highest concentration of homicides in the city with over 400 per year during the early 1990s. The new South Bureau Homicide Unit would centralize all of the homicide investigations to help distribute the workload, pool resources, provide for better communication, and tie together similar cases. In the years that this bureau has been up and running, the clearance rate for homicides improved from 50 percent to 88 percent. There were initially 44 detectives in the four divisions, which has grown to almost 60 for South Bureau. In 1998, there were 157 homicides.

South Bureau Homicide also implemented the first-of-its-kind Community Response Vehicle (CRV) in Los Angeles with the help of federal grant money and local contributions. Purchased in 1996 from Fleetwood Motor Homes, the CRV is a combination motor home, mobile office, and mobile command post.

When a homicide is discovered, the uniformed division secures the scene and notifies the watch commander. The watch commander in turn notifies the South Bureau Unit which calls a team of two detectives and a supervisor to the scene with the CRV.

The CRV runs out of the South Bureau Homicide Unit. It is a mobile home that has been customized to assist during a homicide investigation. Exterior compartments carry forensic tools for the detectives. There is also an awning that can provide a sheltered work area from the rain or hot sun when the unit is moved up to the crime scene.

The front area of the CRV has comfortable chairs, a sofa, galley, and table with booth-type seating on either side. The galley contains a lavatory, sink, refrigerator, microwave oven, television, VCR, and coffee maker, as well as other basic amenities. This area is designed as a lounge for witnesses and family so they can relax and calm down in order to adjust to the crime that just occurred. It allows them some privacy and comfort when they may have no place to go other than remaining on the street or sitting in the back seat of a radio car. The detectives will offer them soda, coffee, and food. They also have towels, blankets, and medical supplies.

In gang-related crimes, the homicide detectives can get witnesses out of sight from others who might threaten retaliation or intimidation.

The rear section is set up as an office with a

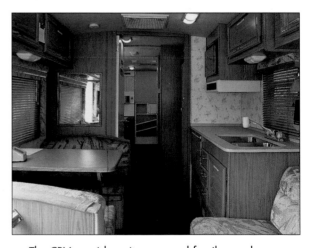

The CRV provides witnesses and family members comfortable quarters and privacy so they can work with the homicide detectives in a non-threatening environment. Blankets, food, and hot or cold drinks go a long way toward helping someone to settle down after a tragic event has occurred.

Mobile 7 is one of two 35-foot Fruehauf trailers that have been specially designed with templates for the SEMS, which is mandated by California state law. There are rooms in the trailer for commanders and for the gathering of information. It is shown here being pulled by one of two 1998 Sterling tractors.

fax, color copier, computer, phones, and desk space. The detectives can conduct interviews here and type their reports. They can perform many duties that would otherwise have to wait until they returned to the police station.

The rear area also has a television and VCR. This allows for the immediate review of store security tapes to identify suspects in a crime. The color copier comes in handy, too, especially when gangs are suspected in the crime. Since each of the gang officers always carries a large book with color photos of suspected and known gang members, the homicide detectives can compile a page of color photos, make copies, and hand them out to patrol officers to begin a quick canvas of witnesses and neighbors. This also aids in the reproduction of photos of an unidentified victim for the same reason.

Other features of the CRV include an outside retractable canopy to provide shade as well as protection from the rain for detectives conducting an investigation. The CRV carries shovels, rakes, ropes, tools, portable floodlights, a 7-kW curbside generator, and a 4-kW roadside generator in the external compartments.

Equipment and supplies inside the unit include metal detectors, fans, biohazard suits, blood kits for the collection of blood samples, a gun residue testing kit, office supplies, and two shotguns for tactical protection.

Uniformed Support Division

Major incidents in the city elicit a response from the LAPD Uniformed Support

Mobile 5 is hooked to a 1992 Volvo tractor with a 14-kW generator mounted behind the cab. This trailer differs from Mobile 7 in several ways. For starters, it has a lower floor and a single rear axle that makes it more difficult to navigate in some sections of the city. It also has two side doors for entry where Mobile 7 has just one.

Division. They are responsible for several pieces of specialized equipment. Among the units they maintain are two portable lighting trailers, a 30-kW mobile generator trailer, two sound trucks, a mobile command post bus, one 30-foot Fruehauf trailer with supplies, four Fruehauf trailers that are set up as command posts, and five over-the-road tractors to pull the trailers. They also have a 16-foot canteen trailer with a stove, refrigerator, and 6.5-kW generator.

The interior of Mobile 5 shows a large open area with multiple positions for staff members. Although there is a small area with a folding partition that is not visible from this view, primary calls for this trailer do not require a separate, private, conference area. This is the unit of choice when the Los Angeles City Fire Department requests a police command trailer.

Mobile 2 is the supply unit and uses a 1969 Fruehauf trailer. Mobile 6 is a 1974 Blue Bird bus chassis and body without the side windows and interior seats. The interior is open and has positions and desks for several people to keep track of the on-scene operations for a large incident. The unit has a 6- and 12-kW generator.

Mobiles 1, 5, and 7 are 35-foot trailers that are outfitted to accommodate more personnel than Mobile 6. The trailers are a 1948 Fruehauf, 1967 Diamond, and 1948 Fruehauf respectively. At a major incident, Mobiles 1 and 7 can be backed together and linked via the rear trailer doors to provide a 70-foot command module. Each trailer also has a side door, and if needed, Mobile 5 can park alongside Mobile 7 and the two can be linked together through the side doors with the use of a ramp.

Mobile 5 has two side doors. The interior contains a single, large compartment with a sliding door that can partition the rear section for a conference area. One of the side doors provides access to this area. This unit is frequently special-called to an incident when the primary need is for a communications center, as opposed to the need for the conference area, and is most often requested by the fire department on joint incidents. This trailer has a lower floor than the others as well as a single rear axle. This makes it less maneuverable than the other units, which have dual rear axles.

Mobiles 1 and 7 have similar interiors. They are both divided into two separate compartments. The front is a command area and the rear is for communications. The command area has large wet boards on each wall to keep track of personnel and other administrative statistics. These boards have been laid out with a template conforming to the Standardized Emergency Management System (SEMS), of which the Incident Command System (ICS) is a component. California state law requires all agencies to use

Each EOD officer has a take-home sport utility vehicle since they rotate 24-hour on-call status. The heavy-duty rollout shelf makes all of the equipment easily accessible. Here, one of LAPD's finest demonstrates a portable x-ray device that is used to screen suspicious luggage or parcels.

the ICS to get reimbursement of funds for incidents involving mutual aid. The basis of the ICS is to provide uniform equipment, supplies, and a command structure to insure unity, standardization, and communication between multiple agencies working together. Briefly, under the ICS, there is a unified command that is made up of the heads of each participating agency, and an incident commander responsible for initiating and executing the orders down through the command structure.

The front compartment of these trailers will accommodate hard-wired phones and has positions for four mobile radio operators. The rear section is for processing information and contains computers, faxes, a copy machine, a TV, phones, and space for six communications personnel and three computer operators.

Pulling these trailers are two 1998 Sterling tractors and a 1990 Freightliner tractor, each with a 25-kW generator mounted behind the cab. A 1991 and a 1992 Volvo tractor complete

The EOD maintains two mechanical robots for investigating and retrieving confirmed or suspected live ordnance devices. Max and Andros live inside this bomb truck, which is special-called to a scene only after bomb techs determine they need it. Inside the truck, an operator will direct either robot by wireless remote control with the help of the cameras mounted on the robots.

the fleet with 15-kW and 14-kW generators respectively.

Approximately 12 times per year all four Mobile command posts are required to handle simultaneous incidents. Roughly six times per year, an incident requires them all at the same scene.

DSD - Explosives Section, the Bomb Squad

The bomb squad is another unit with specialized vehicles and equipment. Each of the 14

explosives technicians is assigned a Chevy Suburban or Tahoe sport utility vehicle as a take-home vehicle. These units are unmarked, though easily recognizable. They are loaded down with all of the basic equipment that a technician will need when responding to an incident with an explosive device. They carry hand and power tools, a bomb suit, a portable x-ray unit, remote disrupter, a recon vest, and ballistic helmet.

The bomb squad also has a dump truck, a bomb truck with robots, a TCV, and a robotic forklift. The TCV is a 1960s-vintage military surplus total containment vessel that is mounted on a GMC 6000 truck chassis that they received from another city department. The vessel has the capacity to withstand a blast equal to 40 pounds of TNT. This unit responds to a scene if a device has to be detonated by the bomb tech within the city limits. Pipe bombs, blasting caps, and dynamite can be detonated with the use of explosives inside the chamber.

The bomb truck that houses the robots has a Chevy chassis and a utility body that has exterior compartments as well as a walk-in area where two robots are stored. The first unit is a TR-2000 enhanced tactical robot called Max. Max weighs 45 pounds and has a 1,000-foot range with the wireless control. It can be configured to pass through less than 5 inches of vertical space and can reach up to 5 feet high. Max can lift between 10 and 30 pounds depending on the extension of the arm and has two cameras onboard. The one in front is a color camera while the rear facing camera is black and white. Max is mainly used for reconnaissance because it is easier to maneuver than the other robot.

The second robot is an Andros model by Remotec that is a 1993-vintage unit. It is an all-terrain, multi-tracked, remote-controlled vehicle for deployment in hostile environments. It weighs over 700 pounds and can travel on wet or dry surfaces. This robot can be controlled with 300 feet of hard wire to a control box or with a wireless line-of-sight control. Andros also has two forward facing color cameras to provide the eyes for the technicians. One camera is static while the other can be rotated from the remote position. Andros has a longer arm with better reach than Max. This robot is used to retrieve a device or suspicious item after the scouting was done by Max.

Any response for the bomb squad includes three people: one supervisor and two working

The TCV uses a chassis that saw service with another city department before being assigned to the EOD. This vessel is rated to withstand a blast equal to 40 pounds of TNT.

techs. Additional techs will be called if one of the special vehicles or explosives are needed. In a long, drawn-out incident, additional techs may be called out to relieve the original on-scene techs, who may be encumbered with fatigue. Whether the scenario involves removing a device or employing a render safe procedure (RSP), standard protocol dictates that for safety, only one tech goes down range during an incident. Working with explosives is dangerous work. Since 1986, the LAPD bomb squad has had two technicians killed and three seriously injured.

The explosives technicians work an 8-hour day with 24-hour rotating on-call shifts. They only respond to incidents where a device has been found or has detonated since they will conduct the post-blast investigation. The LAPD bomb squad averages 1,000 calls per year where a device or suspicious item is found. Roughly 30 to 40 percent turn out to be actual explosive devices. The number one reason for bombings is

The LAPD was the first department in the country to have a SWAT team. They are assigned to the Metropolitan Division as the "D" Platoon. Recently they acquired a new SWAT truck. Although team members respond directly to a scene with their radio car, one member will bring the truck from headquarters. Tactical teams throughout the country invite LAPD SWAT officers to speak to their teams and assist with training.

vandalism, and the number one place all bombings occur is in residences. Pipe bombs are the most common device, with homemade hand grenades being the next most common device.

A canine unit, not the DSD, conducts bomb detection security sweeps with bomb sniffing dogs. The only general exception to this involves dignitary sweeps and bomb threats involving airplanes. The bomb squad will use their portable x-ray equipment to supplement the equipment at the airport to insure a safe environment.

SWAT

The Metro Division is comprised of the canine unit, the mounted unit, and four field platoons of officers. These platoons are deployed for dignitary protection and to back up the geographic divisions with additional manpower to provide assistance wherever it is needed. The "David" platoon is the LAPD SWAT team. This platoon is divided into several elements and consists of 60 officers, 6 sergeants, and 1 lieutenant. They were initially organized in 1969 as the first specially trained tactical team in the United States. They average 120 call-outs per year split evenly between high-risk warrant service and barricaded subjects. Every SWAT officer has two stripes on his or her uniform that signifies him or her as an instructor. Each element of the team has a "plus one" as the element leader under the sergeant. A plus one is an officer who has an additional stripe under the standard two.

SWAT has four special vehicles. They have two V100 armored personnel carriers, a Peacekeeper armored unit, and a brand-new SWAT truck. One V100 is centrally located near the downtown area while the other is located farther north in the valley. These units are four-wheel-drive vehicles with a top speed of 55 miles per hour. The front is fitted for a ram, enabling the V100 to knock down a door without exposing the team members. The housing has three different settings to hold a 6- or 18-foot-long ram, each with a flat plate on the end. The V100 can accommodate 10 officers including the driver. There is a roof hatch for the driver and the front passenger as well as a rear hatch, a roof turret that can revolve 360 degrees, and an access door on each side of the unit. The V100 is powered by a V-8 Chrysler gas engine with a five-speed transmission, and has heavier armament than the Peacekeeper.

Both V100 units were used during the Watts riots to remove victims of gunfire, for recon, and for patrol duties in areas with extensive sniper fire. For the most part, they were kept in the staging area as reactionary vehicles to respond when snipers pinned down officers or civilians.

As of this writing, the Peacekeeper is a new addition to the SWAT arsenal and is being rebuilt for service.

The SWAT truck that the team uses is built on a 1997 Navistar chassis with a Grumman Ohlsen body. The custom work was done by the Mattman Company and includes exterior compartments and a unique interior design. The truck is divided into two areas that can be separated by a sliding partition. The passenger side has two external doors, one in the front and the second just behind the sliding partition. All of the interior walls are wet boards for writing on with additional boards that can be hung on the

An inside look at the rear portion of the LAPD SWAT truck shows meticulous storage for the team's equipment and supplies. Officers carry their personal weapons and gear, and the truck supplements this with specialty and backup supplies.

outside of the truck. This feature was included as a result of the North Hollywood incident in which two suspects in body armor robbed a bank and then began shooting up the neighborhood while trying to make their escape. Officers needed space for diagrams and maps to trace the suspects' path.

The front interior section is for the Crisis Negotiating Team (CNT) that is part of the SWAT team. There are both cellular and hard-wired phone capabilities as well as a portable phone system that enables them to use a throw phone to initiate communications with a suspect. The front section will be staffed by a primary and secondary negotiator in addition to a CNT supervisor, a behavioral science advisor,

The Los Angeles County SWAT van carries backup munitions and entry tools for the team. It also serves as their mobile command post with wet boards for briefings and an interior area for privacy.

and the officer in charge (OIC). They also have a TV and VCR at their disposal.

In the rear section, storage cabinets on both sides of the truck go from the floor almost to the ceiling. Some of the equipment onboard includes bullhorns, various entry equipment like rams, sledgehammers, mirrors on retractable poles, portable lights, and ballistic shields. They also store medical gear, climbing and rappelling gear, and less-lethal sage guns that fire a rubber projectile, which is more powerful than a beanbag round.

Exterior storage contains a generator, a ground ladder, attic ladder, stepladder, tables, and chairs. There is a retractable awning on each side of the truck, a shoreline power hookup, and modular phone jacks. This unit is a totally self-contained vehicle.

The team has EMTs who are SWAT officers with BLS medical training. The tactical uniform

for the team is a Nomex BDU to protect the officers from incendiary devices such as flash bangs.

One type of entry will consist of a five-member unit. The first person will breach the door while the next person, the cover, offers protection and is the first through the door. The third in line will either have an MP-5 or a shotgun. The fourth team member will follow with whichever weapon was not in the hands of the number three team member. After breaching the door, number one will grab his or her entry weapon (which is slung over the shoulder) and drop into line as number five. This scenario will vary depending on the dangers present inside the building.

The LAPD SWAT team prefers to use gas to force a suspect to surrender. They do not encourage long standoffs that would inconvenience an entire neighborhood. Like all teams, they want

The TRV resembles the SWAT van. It also carries cable that is hooked to the rear tow eyes for pulling gates, fences, and security bars. Skids that are stored on the roof of the TRV slide into brackets under the body and provide platforms for team members to stand on for quick deployment.

to go in and arrest the suspect without injury to officers or the suspect.

Los Angeles County

The Los Angeles County Sheriff's Department has a Special Enforcement Bureau (SEB) that encompasses five areas of responsibility. These include the Special Enforcement Detail (SED), the Emergency Services Detail (ESD), the Reserve Motor Detail (RMD), and the canine and mounted units. The SED, ESD, and canine units are permanent full-time deployments, whereas the RMD and mounted units are staffed by deputies from other areas.

SED

The SED is the county's tactical unit. This is a very active team with over 200 deployments during 1998. Although the majority of their deployments were for the execution of high-risk warrants, they also handled a large number of incidents involving barricaded subjects. No shots were fired by the team while resolving any of the situations in 1998.

Two teams, minimum, are on duty or standby at all times. Six teams rotate the active duty schedule that includes daytime patrol when deputies are not training or participating in a call-out. Some situations require a full-bureau activation. These include an officer shooting and hostage scenarios. Large-scale deployments require assembling an arrest team in addition to the entry team, perimeter personnel, and the two-person long gun teams.

The SED uses the arrest team as a crisis entry team during hostage incidents. While the team leaders are formulating plans for an entry, the arrest team deploys quickly and stands ready to intervene if the suspect comes out. If hostages are injured or fired upon, the arrest team can act immediately, going in to resolve the situation and protect the remaining hostages.

When the SED team is activated, some deputies will respond directly to the incident in their radio cars while others are assigned the task of bringing the special deployment vehicles from the SEB headquarters. They have three vehicles: the SWAT van, the Tactical Response Vehicle (TRV), and the Armored Response Vehicle (ARV). Each of the three vehicles is due to respond to the scene of a call-out. In addition, a second ARV is stationed at the north end of the county for deployment there.

The SWAT van has a body with a rear walk-in area and external storage compartments that is mounted on a GMC 3500 HD chassis. It carries additional armaments for the team, rams, pry bars, bomb blankets, road spikes, tear gas canisters with a gun, ladders, and ballistic shields. The van will also act as the command post for the team and has a wet board in an external compartment for notes and diagrams. If a deputy does not want to take a radio car home while on call, his or her equipment will be stored in the SWAT van.

The TRV has a basic truck similar to the SWAT van. They both have small walk-in areas that are accessible from the rear of the units and GMC 3500 Series chassis. The TRV carries more of the same equipment and supplies that are on the SWAT van, but in addition carries cable that can be affixed to a cleat at the rear of the truck to pull gates, fences, and doors from their supports. The sides of the truck's body have fittings to accommodate metal skids that are stored on the roof. These skids can be affixed to either or both sides of the TRV, allowing for a platform to support team members. The TRV can move the team quickly into their primary position to assemble for entry as well as provide cover when they ride on one side and are shielded from the suspects.

The ARV is a military surplus Peacekeeper unit. It is generally kept in reserve at a scene to aid deputies who are taking rounds or to evacuate deputies and civilians who are pinned down by fire and unable to get to a safe position. The ARV has a roof turret that is surrounded by armored plates and permanent skids on three sides for deputies to ride on.

ESD

The ESD currently operates three two-person rescue trucks. They also have several four-wheel-drive sport utility vehicles and a 28-foot boat, in addition to helicopter support from the air services detail. Each member of the ESD is a paramedic and has specialized training to handle all types of emergencies that occur in the mountains and forested areas of the county.

The rescue trucks, which are referred to as "Robert 1, 2, and 3," carry a vast array of equipment and supplies supplemented by personal gear that each deputy has added based on their own personal experiences. They carry oxygen, suction devices, intubation kits, telemetry, and backpacks that serve as their trauma kits with supplies for at least two trauma victims. Rescue gear includes a come-a-long tool, pry bars, chains, hand and power tools, and spare gasoline. The ESD deputies are also divers. Each truck has gear for two divers trained in rescue diving, search diving, high-altitude diving, and cold water diving. The latter two types of diving both greatly decrease the length of time a diver can stay in the water. Each Robert unit also has a surface-supplied-air diving system that allows for communication between the diver and the deputy tethering the line from the surface.

The ESD trucks carry a vast array of equipment and supplies for mountain rescues, water rescues, survival, and medical emergencies. The ESD officers are cross-trained to perform all of these specialized duties in addition to providing the medical support for the SED team.

Other equipment carried onboard includes mountain rescue gear, inclement weather gear, rappelling gear, and swift-water rescue gear such as wet suits, ropes, helmets, and life vests. They carry a stokes basket, snow litter, various splints, backboards, and tactical gear including a ballistic helmet and vest. Whenever the SED deploys, the ESD becomes the medical response team to provide trauma care in the event that a deputy is injured. The ESD will also deploy as part of the entry team at any incident involving hostages.

Generally, two of the Robert units are out during daytime hours performing patrol duties and the third unit is assigned to patrol with the air support unit that is based in Long Beach. In the event of a mountain rescue, seven mountain rescue teams, which are manned by reserve deputies or volunteers, augment the ESD. Each team is fully trained and consists of 20–40 members who deploy rapidly in the event of an emergency. The reserve deputies have all the powers of full-time deputies when they are activated.

41

3
CHAPTER THREE

SPECIAL TEAMS AND DEPARTMENTS

D etroit Metropolitan Airport

R oughly 30 million passengers use the Detroit Metropolitan Airport annually. Located in Wayne County and within the limits of the city of Romulus, security previously was provided through a division of the Wayne County Sheriff's Department. Currently, protection for the airport comes from the 110-person Wayne County Airport Police Department, which is a unique entity. They are responsible for all law enforcement on the airport property with the exception of hands-on security screening of carry-on baggage. Equal in size to many small cities, the airport spans 12 square miles. The airport police also has responsibility for law enforcement at the smaller Willow Run Airport in nearby Ypsilanti. The airport police department has special deployment vehicles assigned to the bomb squad and the Special Response Unit (SRU).

One of the Michigan State Police Department's mobile crime labs is shown along with a bomb tech and a TCV that is capable of withstanding a blast of 10 pounds of TNT. There are seven mobile crime labs throughout the state as well as seven TCVs.

EOD

The bomb squad, also known as the Explosive Ordnance Division (EOD), has a response truck, total containment vessel, and various support vehicles. The response truck is a Chevy Step Van 30 bread truck outfitted with a side ramp. The unit carries all the items necessary for disrupting an explosive device, a portable x-ray unit, a remote controlled robot, "frag bags," and two bomb suits.

The robot, which is capable of going into an airplane, can be controlled remotely with 300+ feet of hard-line cable, or by a radio control. The operator has a console inside the EOD response truck and uses a monitor to view through a camera mounted on the robot.

With the heightened state of alertness at the airport, the EOD team is constantly called to evaluate suspicious bags throughout the terminals. Phoned-in bomb threats also keep them busy. Airlines first evaluate the threats that are phoned-in to them. Then, the first line of defense is to inspect the aircraft using trained dogs. Searching a large plane will thoroughly fatigue a dog.

The EOD team will work with the checked bags while the dog starts in the plane's cabin. The operation involves evacuating passengers and removing carry-on bags to run them through the x-ray machines again. The EOD will bring a vehicle with a large x-ray machine to the site and examine all the checked bags. They look for such items as a power source, wires, and blasting caps.

Basic procedures vary depending on the level of threat and the device that is discovered. For small items, a team member will suit up and use a hot stick to pick up the device and place it into a frag bag for transport to a safe spot for detonation. The frag bag is a specially reinforced container that will contain fragments from a small device like a pipe bomb or hand grenade during transport if it detonates prematurely.

The EOD will respond off the airport property roughly once a month to handle a live device. Most often these consist of hand grenades, pipe bombs, homemade fireworks, and items commonly referred to as "McGyver bombs." Kids having fun are responsible for the McGyver bombs, homemade devices similar to the concoctions made famous by the television show. Similarly, gangs (or curious thrillseekers) assemble pipe bombs. After they've built a pipe bomb, it is common for people to test their creation in an open field. When and if they do not detonate, the bombs are left in the field until someone happens upon them. The EOD will safely disrupt them so that no one gets hurt.

SRU

The SRU continually trains to take action in worst-case scenarios in the event of a terrorist attack at the airport. They utilize a close quarter battle facility (CQB) on the airport grounds along with an obstacle course for conditioning, an explosive entry section, shotgun breaching area, and a five-story-rappelling tower. The team incorporates medics from the fire department in addition to negotiators for a total of 18 members. One medic will make entry with the team at the back of the line, remaining behind cover to be called up as needed with a trauma bag.

Their vehicles include a response truck and a supply trailer. The trailer has been custom built to accommodate an array of specialized tools and equipment. They have 12 aluminum ladders that were designed for tactical use. The ladders are lightweight and can be used in varying lengths. They can be assembled side by side so that several team members can enter a plane or building simultaneously. Accessories include cushions for the ladder tips, which allow them to be quietly placed against an aircraft without alerting hostile subjects inside. Also in the trailer are ballistic shields, battering rams, saws, and cutting torches.

The Detroit Airport EOD response truck houses their radio-controlled robot. One unusual bomb-related incident that occurred at the airport involved an international passenger who spoke poor English. Realizing that he was on the wrong plane, he left and tried to board a second plane, then he got off the second plane. This behavior was deemed suspicious, so both planes were evacuated and searched. Since both flights were international, each aircraft was large. It takes roughly three hours to search a DC-10. In the end, after being able to properly communicate with the passenger, it was discerned that he was merely confused about which was the appropriate flight.

The response truck is built on a GMC 6500 chassis with a custom body by the Mattman Company. Inside the truck are sliding gun racks for 15 MP-5s, additional racks for long guns, shotgun storage in drawers, enough benches to accommodate the entire team, and an onboard radio repeater. They have a unique radio system capable of cross-patching six different radio systems on-scene, allowing everyone to use their own radios at multi-jurisdictional incidents.

The majority of SRU responses occur off airport property providing mutual aid to other agencies with barricaded subjects and hostage incidents.

Michigan State Police

Michigan is the eighth most populated state in the United States with a population of 9,295,297 people. Michigan has a state police department (MSP) that was established in March of 1919. It originated during World War I as a temporary emergency force called the Michigan State Troops that was organized like a military cavalry unit. The Michigan State Troops had about 300 "troopers" to handle security in the state while the National Guard was fighting in the war. Following the military rank structure that was in place with the Troops, the director of the MSP was given the rank of colonel. Today, the MSP has close to 1,300 troopers who handle highway patrol duties along with criminal

The SRU response truck is the mobile command post for SRU operations. It is equipped with an onboard radio repeater and a radio system that allows cross patching of six different radio systems to simplify multi-agency communications. Here, the SRU truck is set up at their training facility complete with a five-story rappelling tower. Fire department medics have been trained to work with the SRU and have become part of the team.

Inside the Detroit Metropolitan Airport SRU truck there are slide-out storage racks for 15 MP-5s, lockers for each team member's tactical gear, and lower drawers for shotgun storage. The red lighting is used to allow officers to enter and exit the truck during nighttime ops without having to adjust from bright lights to the darkness.

investigations throughout the state. The MSP cooperates with local and federal agencies for criminal matters and traffic safety. They participate in the Violent Crimes Task Force, a multi-jurisdictional fugitive apprehension team and a multi-jurisdictional drug team, to share information, investigate crimes, and apprehend fugitive felons.

Due to Michigan's size and diversity, the MSP is organized to provide its entire range of standard and specialized services to citizens all over the state. To accomplish this, the MSP has divided the state into seven districts that encompass 63 posts. Some posts may accommodate as few as one or two troopers, while others are

home for many troopers in addition to specialized vehicles, technicians, and teams. Most of the special vehicles are assigned to the Emergency Support Team (EST), the bomb squad, command and communications, mobile crime labs, and the canine units.

Forensics plays a large part in the criminal investigations that the MSP handles, and in 1996, they were accredited by the American Society of Crime Lab Directors. At the cutting edge of forensic sciences, the MSP has seven labs plus nine satellite locations for polygraph testing. They provide state-of-the-art analysis on criminal investigations for agencies throughout Michigan. These labs handle more than 58,000 cases annually including over 200 crime scene locations and more than 300 bomb and explosive device calls. The MSP forensics labs also work with the Combined DNA Index System (CODIS) integrating DNA records into a national database. Michigan law allows for the collection of DNA samples from both convicted and paroled sex offenders, juvenile felons, convicted murderers and those convicted of attempted murder. Currently, they collect over 3,000 DNA samples a year.

There are seven mobile crime lab vehicles located at posts throughout the state. These units respond to accident and crime scenes with three or four technicians. They provide latent fingerprint detection and identification, firearm identification, crime scene photography, and the use of chemical re-agents to locate evidence and trace evidence at crime scenes. Most of the vehicles for the mobile crime labs are pickup truck chassis with basic utility bodies. The technicians store most of the equipment they'll need at a crime scene in the truck, while the balance of specialized equipment will travel with individuals in their own vehicles.

The bomb squad has seven TCVs throughout the state. One is a top-vent unit while the other

The MSP also operates helicopters and a canine unit with dogs and handlers located throughout the state. Most of the dogs are "bite" dogs that have secondary training in either drugs or explosives. These are supplemented with tracking dogs for both live and dead subjects.

six load from the side. A TCV built by Nabco is located centrally at the state police headquarters compound in East Lansing. The chamber has the capacity to withstand a blast equal to 10 pounds of TNT. The chamber is mounted to a trailer that is pulled behind a Chevy Suburban. The Suburban is fitted with a heavy shelf that can roll out the rear doors. The shelf is loaded with equipment and supplies for the bomb technicians stored in bags, boxes, and toolboxes. The bomb squad answers between 350 and 400 explosives-related calls per year. Roughly 60 of these calls are assigned to the unit that responds from the compound. Much of their duty is to "render-safe" improvised explosive devices and the occasional unexploded military ordnance.

The MSP EST is divided into several teams around the state. The unit assigned to the compound in East Lansing has the newest response truck. Whenever one team is called out, a second team is placed on standby as a backup or relief team depending on the need. Here, a marksman in urban camouflage checks his weapon before storing it in the truck.

The interior of the EST truck shows bench seating, a small desk, and several storage compartments for ballistic shields, ground covers for the snipers, reload ammunition, and specialized weapons.

The NIPAS EST entry team conducts a briefing before completing their mission. The wet board that mounts on the outside of the truck allows them to meet without interfering with the command personnel inside the vehicle.

The EST is the state police's tactical unit. Similar to other MSP specialized units, the EST is spread into teams around the state and trains for situations involving hostage rescue, barricaded gunmen, high-risk arrest and search warrant service, VIP security, and counter terrorism. Averaging 125 call-outs annually, the closest team will be called into action while a secondary team may be put on standby to assist or relieve the primary team for long events. Each team has an EST truck to respond with specialized equipment and supplies. They also maintain an armored vehicle to protect officers taking fire. The newest unit assigned to the EST has a custom-designed Supreme Body which is mounted on a 1996 Ford F Series chassis. The unit has a large generator in an exterior compartment and the interior section has storage space along with a desk. Although most team members carry their armaments in their state-owned patrol vehicles, various backup munitions and specialized weapons are stored in the truck. Also onboard are ballistic shields, tactical mirrors, and ground covers to provide insulation for snipers or observers to use in foul weather.

The state police also maintains a mobile command vehicle (MCV) stationed at the compound. Available to respond anywhere in Michigan in a matter of hours, this state-of-the-art unit leaves few details undone. The MCV is equipped to handle any type of emergency that may occur. The truck has a 1998 International chassis with a Grumman Ohlsen body that was outfitted by LDV. Some of the vehicle's highlights include a conference room, a bathroom, and a kitchenette with a sink, microwave, and refrigerator. For communications, the MCV has four separate positions with radios utilizing 800 MHz, VHF, UHF, and low-band frequencies to coordinate multi-agency incidents. There are televisions, VCRs, cable TV, and a satellite dish to monitor local and national media coverage of events. Additionally, telephones, fax machines, computers, a copier, and printer are onboard to assemble the data needed to efficiently manage the incident. The computers onboard can access the MSP mainframe at the compound. The roof is equipped with two closed circuit cameras that can be controlled from inside the vehicle, allowing officials to monitor and record events going on outside.

Remote regions with limited access to the technical resources required to effectively manage a large scale incident will especially benefit from the MCV.

The MSP MCV interior is equipped with radios, TVs, VCRs, telephones, and computer equipment. It can be partitioned into four separate areas that include the galley and the rear conference area. LDV in Milwaukee built the custom cabinets and handled the wiring and equipment installation.

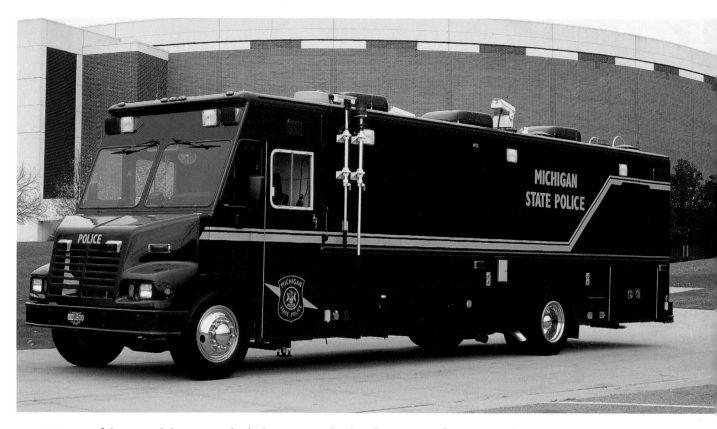

MSP's state-of-the-art mobile command vehicle is equipped to handle any type of emergency that may occur. Stationed centrally at the compound, it can be anywhere in the state in a matter of hours. It will be especially useful in the remote regions of the state that have limited access to the technical resources that are required to effectively manage a large-scale incident.

Northern Illinois Police Alarm System

Many departments require the services of a tactical team but do not have the staff or resources to maintain, outfit, and train a full team. Some rely on neighboring departments while others call on the county or state response teams to handle incidents within their jurisdictions. An alternative to this situation was implemented in Northern Illinois. In an attempt to keep overall control of a situation that would be turned over to the state or county teams when they arrive, many local departments have pooled their resources to form the North

ern Illinois Police Alarm System (NIPAS). Member departments of NIPAS are in two counties and vary in size from 14 to over 100 officers each. The geographical area of NIPAS covers 280 square miles with a population nearing one million. NIPAS provides several functions for these departments. One is the NIPAS Car Plan that covers preplanning of multi-departmental mutual aid responses to assist each department when they have a need for additional personnel for events such as traffic at a large incident, a manhunt for a fugitive, or help with a disaster.

On-scene at a call-out for a barricaded subject, the NIPAS EST truck is in position at the staging area within the outermost perimeter. Command personnel work in the front area while tactical officers check out gear from the rear storage section.

NIPAS also formed the Emergency Services Team (EST); a part-time tactical unit made up of officers from each member department. These officers train for deployment when a high-risk critical incident arises and the local shift commander requests tactical assistance. Each officer responds from their respective department whether they are off duty or working during their regular shift. On duty, they will carry tactical gear in their patrol car and respond "hot" directly to the call-out. Off duty, they can go to their station for a car or respond in their own vehicle. Officers will don their tactical

gear when they arrive on-scene. The EST is divided into seven team elements: tactical command, entry, perimeter, marksmen, negotiations, tactical emergency medical support (TEMS), and support services. Warrant Service is an additional team that is comprised of select officers from the seven teams already mentioned. This element executes the high-risk warrants.

The NIPAS EST has a command and equipment vehicle that was one of the first of its kind to be constructed by LDV. It is built on an International chassis with a Grumman Ohlsen body, that has an overall length of 35 feet. The interior was custom designed by the team members and implemented by LDV. The truck is divided into two sections. The front is the command and communications area that does not connect to the rear. There are positions for three people with radios, a combination fax and copy machine, a computer, an ALERTS terminal for police record searches, and a remote video monitoring system. At a call-out for a barricaded subject, a radio officer, log officer, and a tactical command officer will staff this area.

The rear area is accessible through a door at the back of the vehicle. This is the armory and supply center. Some of the equipment carried here includes ballistic blankets, hand-held lanterns, wet boards, and less-lethal munitions along with Sage guns and shotguns for less-lethal deployment. The truck also has power cords with portable lights, various entry tools, tear gas and guns, a breaching shotgun, diversionary devices, communications gear, and medical supplies for the TEMS officers. The EST has hand-held ballistic shields, a Level III shield on wheels, and a custom-made Level IV shield to offer varying degrees of protection from armed suspects. On the outside of the truck, there is an awning for protection from the sun or rain, a generator, mounting brackets for the wet boards, and several additional storage compartments.

The NIPAS EST has been in force for 12 years and averages 6–10 incidents annually that involve barricaded subjects, armed suicidal subjects, or hostage incidents in addition to several high-risk warrant missions. To date, a barricaded gunman has fired upon them at just one incident. To resolve this mission, the marksman element was compelled to use lethal force. The balance of their assignments have been concluded through peaceful negotiations or covert entry followed by the arrest of the subjects.

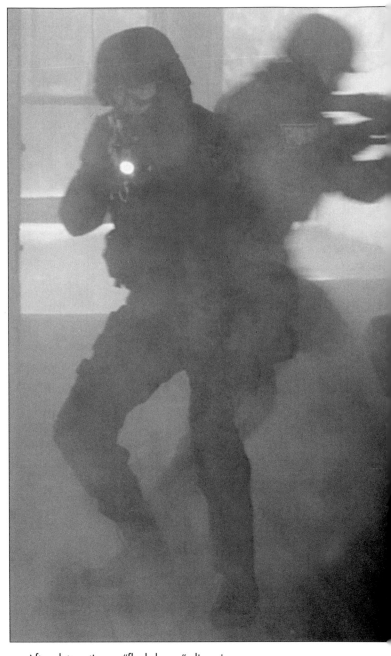

After detonating a "flash-bang" diversionary device, the NIPAS EST entry team advances into a house looking for bad guys. In this case, they came up empty except for the photographer that they hassled just for the heck of it.

CHAPTER FOUR

COUNTY DEPARTMENTS

Miami-Dade County, Florida

Dade County covers approximately 2,200 square miles with a population in excess of 2 million. The Miami-Dade Police Department is responsible for patrolling roughly 1,200 square miles of the total. The department has over 2,900 sworn officers and 1,600 civilians.

Since the mid-1980s, the Miami-Dade Police Department has maintained a full-time Special Response Team (SRT) to handle barricaded subjects, hostage incidents, high-risk warrant service, and other critical risk incidents.

The bomb squad's remote-controlled Hare robot prepares to place a device into the TCV. A small shelf rolls out of the TCV to hold the device.

The Miami-Dade SRT has twin trucks for deployment of the team. Built on Ford F-700 Series chassis, the body provides space for a team to travel during their shift. Officers load their personal gear into the truck when their tour of duty begins, and they stay together as a unit throughout the shift.

The SRT is a very active team executing over 196 warrants in 1998 in addition to handling 20 barricaded subjects, 5 suicides, 2 incidents with hostages, 25 dignitary protection details, and 54 canine and tactical and narcotics team (T&T) raids. The SRT has three special vehicles for the team's use. They have two "trucks" and a wrecker. The two trucks are identical 1991 Ford F700s with walk-in bodies by EVF of Florida. Each unit is used to transport a team and their equipment. They carry various hand tools, axes, bolt cutters, an attic ladder, and an extension ladder. There are entry tools that include pry

bars, a sledgehammer, and a halogen tool. The truck's body has double doors in the back and a single door on the side. During the execution of a search or arrest warrant, the entry team will often use the side door for deployment while the perimeter team will exit via the rear. The crew area can seat the entire team on benches that provide underneath storage space. Additional equipment onboard includes tactical mirrors, ballistic shields and blankets, rappelling gear, and night vision gear. Each officer carries personal gear and weapons in a patrol vehicle and loads them into the truck for each shift.

The wrecker provides the SRT with the greatest amount of fun. It is with this unit that they destroy fences, gates, and personal security systems to allow the team members to execute an arrest warrant.

The "wrecker" is a modified light-duty tow truck on a 1995 Ford F Series Super Duty chassis. In place of the boom and traditional wrecker body, the rear section is outfitted with handrailings on both sides and up the middle. This enables a fully outfitted team to ride in the back to move up during a critical incident or to execute a warrant and deploy rapidly. The front of the wrecker has a push bumper and steel frame for ramming fences and large gates. There are two tow hooks in the front and rear as well as a rear-mounted 12,000-pound winch. These items come in handy when executing a "pull" to remove iron security bars from doors and windows.

The bomb squad is also a full-time unit, consisting of a sergeant and five officers. Each team member has a "take-home" van while the sergeant has a Chevy Suburban. Each van contains x-ray equipment, bomb suits, de-armers, and tool kits. One officer is responsible for the team's Hare wheeled robot and carries two ramps to deploy the robot from within the van. The Hare is remote controlled by 500 feet of fiber optic cable. The unit has three cameras, one on the arm, one to drive the unit, and the other with pan and tilt capabilities. There is a speaker and a microphone on the robot so it can be used to communicate with a hostile subject. The Hare can also record the sounds it hears. It has a remote-controlled arm that can extend approximately 6 feet high and a claw at the end capable of rotating 360 degrees.

In addition to each officer's van, the team maintains two large trucks with containment vessels. One has a top-venting vessel while the

The public education unit of the Miami-Dade Police Department uses this tractor-trailer combination to educate people, especially adolescents, about the dangers of driving while impaired. There is a dark window on the other side of the trailer that opens to allow people to observe what is going on inside.

other has a TCV. The TCV is in the back of a utility body that is mounted on a 1988 Chevrolet medium-duty chassis. There is a lift gate at the rear of the truck and storage compartments for post-blast investigation equipment, various tools, and other supplies to supplement each officer. The TCV came with a factory rating to withstand a blast of 10 pounds of C-4 explosives with total containment, whereas the top-vent unit will direct the effects of a blast upwards, out of the vessel. In the center of the TCV chamber is a small slide-out tray to hold any device

that is to be transported to a safer location. This is suspended in the center of the chamber to equalize the effects throughout the entire vessel if a blast occurs.

The team responds to over 200 calls per year involving suspicious packages. More than 20 percent of those incidents result in some type of actual explosive device.

Through a grant from a federal entitlement called the Weed and Seed Program, the Miami-Dade Police Department was able to acquire a used mass transit bus from the regional transportation authority for use in the Northside District. This 1980 GMC model RTS bus had run over 700,000 miles before it was retired. It is currently powered by its sixth eight-cylinder Detroit Diesel engine and was totally rehabbed at the Pride State Prison in Daytona, Florida. A prisoner rehab program provided the labor for the electrical work, carpentry, all of the upholstery, and the installation of the generator. Parts and labor for the rehab totaled $49,500.

The front area of the bus has four workstations containing desks with computer access, a small galley with a refrigerator and microwave, police radios, copier, fax, satellite phone, a bench for the comfort of civilians, and storage for the forms and paperwork that are part of the daily regimen of any police officer.

The bus also is used for special events or any emergency mobilization that would require the use of a command post. The rear section of the bus has its own external door. There is a command post with a conference area, a computer, cell phones, a TV and VCR, and a workstation for one officer with police radios.

Externally, there is a 10-kW diesel generator that runs off the bus' fuel tank, compartment storage for folding tables and chairs, a shoreline power hookup, scene lights on both sides, a retractable awning, tripods with portable quartz lights, and three rooftop central HVAC units. Since most of the windows have been replaced with solid walls, there are two wide-angle cameras located on the outside of the bus to assist the driver.

The Weed and Seed bus is primarily a mobile precinct and outreach center for the public that also serves as a unit for the deterrence of crime. When deployed, it provides a resource for field units, allowing officers to file reports and conduct routine business without having to travel to the precinct headquarters. The bus also follows crime trends to provide a greater police presence in areas with growing or excessive

Inside the vehicle, participants can wear goggles that simulate impairment while they attempt to walk a straight line. There are also video games that simulate impaired driving. Museum-type exhibits illustrate past and present tools used to detect excessive blood alcohol levels.

crime rates. Parked in a prominent public setting, the bus will have in attendance a number of squad cars driven by officers working inside, in addition to the field units that come to take advantage of the convenience. The presence of a mobile unit surrounded by police cars is a deterrence to crime wherever the bus is deployed.

Oakland County Sheriff's Department, Michigan

Oakland County is located north of Detroit. The Sheriff's Department has more than 1,000 paid employees and volunteers. The county encompasses roughly 900 square miles with 1.2 million residents and is totally landlocked. With that said, the Sheriff's Department has a Marine Safety Section of the Protective Services Division that performs underwater search and rescue. They provide regular patrols of the 24 major lakes in the county, while the balance of the 450 lakes are patrolled randomly, making this one of the busiest marine units in the state of Michigan. They have a full-time staff of 7 who are supplemented by more than 30 part-time

The Miami-Dade Police Department uses this converted transit bus as a mobile police station. It is used as a local resource for districts as well as a means to provide greater police presence in troubled areas.

employees. The marine unit maintains 28 patrol boats of various sizes, all-terrain vehicles (ATVs), snowmobiles, and jet skis or Personal Water Crafts (PWCs), along with a Chevrolet Step Van with equipment for the underwater search and rescue operations.

The Protective Services Division also coordinates the department's Special Response Team, a SWAT-type unit. The team utilizes two vehicles: a nondescript box truck for supplies and equipment and a unique armored person-

nel carrier. Built by AV Technology, a General Dynamics Company, the unit is a Dragoon Patroller 2. First seen as a prototype in the movie *Robo Cop*, this unit has the capabilities of traveling on- and off-road in addition to being amphibious. Oakland County currently has the only such unit in the Northern Hemisphere. Weighing in at a hefty 29,000 pounds, it is powered by a turbo-charged 300-horsepower Detroit Diesel 6V-53T engine through an MT653 five-speed Allison automatic transmission. The operator has the option of choosing two- or four-wheel drive and can travel at speeds up to 70 miles per hour on land and roughly three knots in the water. The wheels propel the unit through water, allowing it to swim without touching the bottom.

There is a central tire inflation system (CTIS) so that the driver can regulate the air in the tires to adjust for optimal traction depending on the driving surface. In addition, if the tires are shot out, the driver can travel at 25 miles per hour for approximately 50 miles to relocate the vehicle for the safety of the team or to transport it to an area for service.

The Dragoon Patroller 2 can carry 10–12 officers in a heated and air-conditioned interior. There are hatch-style doors on either side of the vehicle with an additional rear hatch for egress of the team while remaining behind the protection of the unit. The roof is equipped with three hatches: one for the driver, a second for the other crew member, and the third in the center for the team. The unit has exterior compartments for supplemental equipment that the team may require and can be fitted with a ram, push bumper, plow, or lights. Oakland County has set up their unit with a retracting front push bumper that can extend to an overall width of 15 feet to clear a wide path through an unfriendly crowd. In the closed position it measures 8 feet wide.

The Special Response Team is made up of 25 officers who are trained instructors in defensive tactics, tactical command, sniper tactics, explosive entry procedures, gas deployment, special purpose vehicle operation, rappelling, less-than-lethal tactics, special weapons, and hostage negotiations. They have responded to natural disasters and plane crashes in addition to suicidal subjects, hostage situations, barricaded gunmen, and drug raids. The team also has a medical support team working directly

The interior of the Miami-Dade Weed and Seed bus has space for four officers to work, a seating area for citizens, and a rear conference area.

with the unit staffed by tactical medics, doctors, paramedics, trauma nurses, and a psychiatrist for negotiations.

Since the team has employed the Dragoon Patroller 2, they have not been fired upon nor have they had to use lethal force. Once the bad guys see the team approaching in the armored vehicle, they often see the sense in surrendering.

One highly publicized incident that required the Special Response Team occurred in November of 1996 at the Ford Motor Plant in Wixom, Michigan. A camouflaged subject entered the facility, killed a supervisor and wounded two Oakland County Sheriff's officers. The subject fired numerous rounds and a siege ensued. Response team members were able to locate the subject in a sewer system on the grounds and apprehended him using the armored

Oakland County's Marine Unit Safety Section operates this Chevrolet Step Van with gear for several divers. It has a trailer hitch to pull any of the PWCs, snowmobiles, ATVs, or one of the 28 boats that they use for patrol and rescue duties.

An interior view of the Dragoon Patroller 2 shows the driver's area and the position for a unit commander with access to the radios. In the foreground are some of the vents to circulate heat and air conditioning.

unit without the use of lethal force or further injury to officers or the offender.

A sticker placed on the side of the vehicle represents every mission that the Dragoon Patroller 2 has responded to. At the time of this writing, the number of missions, all successful, totaled 21.

Orange County, Florida

The Orange County Sheriff's Office in Central Florida has a 40 member, part-time SWAT team as part of the overall force of 1,200 sworn officers. The team is broken down into two 18-member elements plus supervisory personnel. They average 12 call-outs per year and executed 162 warrants in 1998. The team has four special vehicles which include a van for transporting team members, a command post, and two armored units. The first is an unmarked, extended Ford Econoline van to assist with deployments at an incident. The van carries some of the team's tactical mirrors as well as diversionary devices.

The command post is built on a 1999 Ford F450 chassis. Mounted on the back is a walk-in body built by the Rescue Master Body Co. This is a command post for SWAT personnel. There is seating in the rear to accommodate up to 10 officers in order to conduct briefings. It is equipped with a generator, a retractable awning, and several external storage compartments with basic supplies to allow team members access without going inside and possibly disrupting command operations. Radio batteries,

Oakland County's Dragoon Patroller 2 armored vehicle is the only one of its kind in the Northern Hemisphere. The front push bumper is displayed, extended to its full 15 feet, for clearing a path through an unfriendly crowd.

ballistic shields, night vision equipment, ghillie suits for camouflage, chemical agents, a collapsible ladder, and a briefing board are stored in the exterior compartments. Inside the vehicle, there are phones, radios, a fax machine, and a work area for the command staff. The Crisis Negotiating Team (CNT) is a separate entity and has its own vehicle.

Another new unit for the Orange County team is an M-113A armored personnel carrier.

Next Page
A rear door of the unit is often used for egress of the team. There is a seat at this position that is occupied by the tactical medic who opens the door for the assembled team when they are ready to exit the vehicle. Since the medic brings up the end of the entry team, he or she can exit the vehicle behind the other team members and secure the door.

The Orange County Sheriff's Office SWAT team utilizes this new command vehicle as a base for tactical operations command personnel during the deployment of the team. Basic equipment and supplies are stored in exterior compartments to allow access to officers without disturbing the team leaders inside.

This tracked vehicle was built by FMC in 1962 for the U.S. Army. Later, it was refitted for use by the Israelis, before being acquired and completely restored by a private individual. It is 100 percent armored aluminum, weighs 22,700 pounds, and is powered by a 361 Chrysler gasoline engine. The M-113A has a top speed of 40 miles per hour in sixth gear, can seat a crew of 10 including the driver, and is fully amphibious with a maximum speed of 3 miles per hour in the water. The side gun ports were not part of the original design, but were added by the Israeli Army. It is equipped with night vision gear and has a 360-degree rotating top turret, a rear roof hatch, a rear door, and a rear drop gate. Deployment options include blocking a road or driveway during a mission to prevent suspects from fleeing. It can also provide additional armored cover for team members in a hostile environment to retrieve a downed or pinned officer. It is affectionately nicknamed the Y2K vehicle for its feared deployment during the much-hyped year 2000 mayhem.

The fourth vehicle for the SWAT team is their custom-designed Hummer. Believed to be the first armored Hummer in the country, this vehicle has Level V ballistic plating throughout. All of the glass, the top, the bottom, and the sheet-metal sides are armored. Built on a 1997 two-door Hummer pickup truck, the rear was constructed by the Chicago Armor and Limousine Company. The body portion has seating for 11 fully operational SWAT officers. There is a roof turret with protection on three sides, gun ports on all four sides, and a rear drop plate to protect officers' legs from ground fire if they are walking behind the vehicle. The Hummer features a CTIS to inflate or deflate the tires while the vehicle is moving in order to improve traction.

There is storage under the rear bench seats for entry tools and snatch hooks for pulling fences and security bars. The front of the Hummer has a 12,000-pound winch and is set up to accommodate a 6- or 8-foot ram for knocking down doors and fences. There is also additional front plating to protect the engine and the radiator. The Hummer will deploy to all incidents including warrant service and was designed to rescue officers or civilians who are pinned down by gunfire and unable to get to safety.

This 1962 M-113A armored personnel carrier has been affectionately nicknamed the Y2K vehicle. Although the SWAT team has not had the need to deploy this vehicle as of the writing of this book, it will be ready to address the doomsday mayhem that is being forecast to occur when we usher in the year 2000.

The M-113A can seat a crew of 10 including the driver and is fully amphibious with a maximum speed of 3 miles per hour in the water. The side gun ports were not part of the original design, but were added by the Israeli Army. It is equipped with night vision gear and has a 360-degree rotating top turret, a rear roof hatch, a rear door, and a rear drop gate.

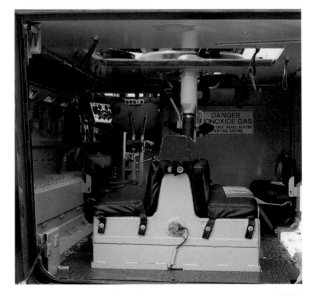

The first deployment for the Hummer was to assist another agency that had one officer killed and another wounded in a gun battle. The officer, who eventually died, was in the open and needed to be rescued. As the Hummer responded with a small team to rescue the downed officer through the rear door, the suspect fired multiple rounds, hitting the hood. Officers put down suppressive fire from the vehicle to prevent the subject from further engaging the team with hostile fire until the injured officer was moved to a safe location.

Westchester County, New York

Westchester County is located north of New York City. The Westchester County Department of Public Safety employs 231 sworn officers and 56 civilian personnel. They are responsible for patrolling 16,000 acres, which include 66 miles of parkways that provide a vital link between New York City and the suburbs of Westchester.

The county police have a Special Services Unit that provides support services including marine rescues and the extrication of persons trapped in vehicles. They also have an aviation unit, motorcycle unit, canine unit, bomb squad, and Special Response Team (SRT). The bomb squad rendered safe 14 explosive devices during 1997 and responded to 16 calls for the securing of explosives.

The Westchester County communications unit has a state-of-the-art command and communications vehicle. Union City built the body and the interior was custom designed and outfitted by LDV. The truck features a 1996 International model 1652SC chassis with a GVW of 28,000 pounds, a wheelbase of 270 inches, and an overall length of 456 inches. It has an International 444E, 210-horsepower, high-torque turbo-charged diesel engine and an Allison AT-545 heavy-duty four-speed automatic transmission.

The command unit includes a 20-kW diesel generator with several cord reels to supply power at an incident. The generator also provides power to control all of the onboard computers, phone equipment, and video equipment. Externally there are 500-watt quartz lights on telescoping poles to illuminate the area around the truck as well as eight halogen lamps mounted directly to the sides of the truck. Outside the vehicle, a 23-foot retractable awning is on one side to provide protection from the elements for personnel working outdoors. They also have a solid enclosure to surround the space under the awning like a tent.

Communication capabilities include multiple land-mobile satellite telephones located in both the conference and communication sections of the vehicle. There is also a phone system with 12 separate lines accessible through 10 phones throughout the inside and outside of the truck. Two-way radio communication equipment includes seven VHF mobile radios capable of scanning 99 channels along with five UHF radios with the same scanning capabilities. The communications area also has a low-band radio, an aviation radio, a marine radio, and an additional tactical radio, along with four miles of wire on spools.

Computer equipment includes several laptops and a combination fax, copier, and printer, along with network sharing capabilities. Video equipment for monitoring the media as well as events outside the unit includes a telescoping mast with a camera through the truck's roof, several microwave video/audio receivers and printers, video recorders and players, editing equipment, and a time-lapse VCR. There are three TV monitors as well as multiple antenna and cable inputs. The vehicle's roof has a reinforced observation/work platform with an access ladder mounted at the rear.

Another special deployment vehicle used by the Westchester County Police SRT is their Light Armored Vehicle (LAV). This unique unit, known as an LAV-25, is the only one of its kind in civilian use in the United States. Over 2,000 of these units were produced by General Motors in Canada for use by the Saudi Arabia National Guard during Desert Storm. Currently, the Marine Corps uses the LAV-25.

Two models of this vehicle are manufactured. A Type I has a turret and is designed for warfare. Some of its features include night vision and provisions for battle during nuclear or biological warfare. The Type II version is an armored personnel carrier. It has the ability to

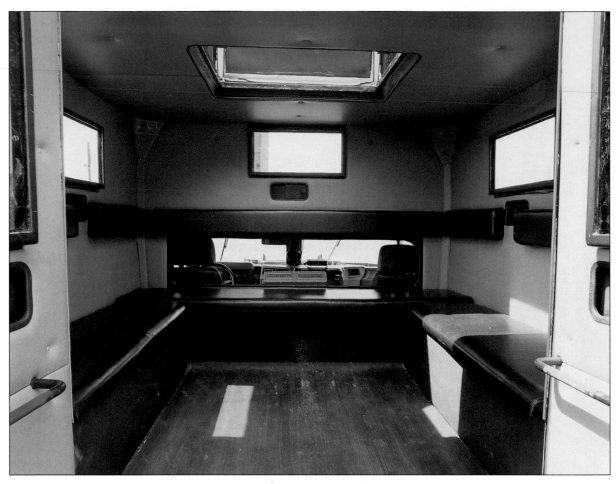

The interior of the Hummer provides bench seating for up to 11 officers who are protected by Level V armored plating. Windows on each side permit the team to survey their surroundings before deploying.

climb as well as amphibious capabilities to maneuver in up to 6 feet of water.

The FBI Hostage Rescue Team (HRT) leased an LAV-25 Type II for riots and other dangerous incidents where team members were under fire. It was painted to match their other vehicles and was taken to the 1996 Montana Freemen situation. When the FBI decided not to renew their lease, the unit had 4,000–5,000 miles on it. The manufacturer refurbished it, and Westchester was then able to obtain this vehicle and adapt it for civilian police use.

The LAV-25 has eight wheels and can travel at speeds up to 70 miles per hour on land and 6 miles per hour in the water. It has constant four-wheel drive and can be switched to eight-wheel drive on demand with an air-over hydraulic system that allows all four of the front wheels to turn. Unlike track units, this LAV does not have to be trailered. It can be driven directly to the scene where it is needed. A six-cylinder, turbo-charged Detroit Diesel engine with an Allison five-speed manual transmission that has five forward and two

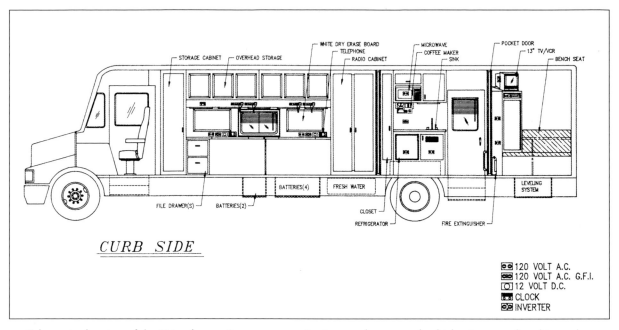

Schematic drawing of the Westchester County communications and command vehicle. Among other things, the unit is equipped with a lavatory and galley for extended operations. The galley includes a refrigerator, microwave, coffee maker, sink, water cooler, and a hot water heater.

reverse gears powers the LAV-25. It can travel up to 850 miles on a single tank of gas.

Inside, the LAV-25 can accommodate two drivers and as many as 12 team members. Ballistic capabilities allow protection from 7.62-mm ammunition. Its overall length is 21 feet, and the unit weighs just over 26,000 pounds. For access and egress, there are six roof hatches as well as a rear door and a hydraulic rear ramp. This particular unit received an additional 1/2-inch-thick armor plating, giving the unit ballistic protection up to a 50-caliber round. The LAV has a 15,000-pound front-end winch and is capable of traveling up to five miles at 30 miles per hour if all of the tires are shot out. Currently, Westchester uses the LAV an average of four times per year, and has never been fired upon to date.

This particular unit has been modified as a prototype unit with the ability to produce a smoke screen. With the flip of an interior switch, the driver can dump raw fuel into the exhaust side of the turbo-charger and create enough of a nontoxic blue/white smoke screen to bury a large building in smoke.

Centrally located, the LAV can be deployed to any location in the county in under an hour. The tactical team consists of 15 members that include patrol officers, detectives, and lieutenants. The SRT is at the disposal of all police agencies in the county. When there is a call-out, the team heads to county police headquarters where they assemble, dress, receive weapons, and then respond to the incident. The LAV deploys from headquarters while the communications and command unit responds from the police academy.

One call-out for the LAV involved a distraught individual who shot and killed two

family members while at home. Local police called the county tactical team who responded with the LAV and the command unit. Two neighboring SWAT teams also responded to the scene. It was not known if one of the victims was still alive and being held against her will, or if a double homicide had occurred.

Local patrol officers had taken positions around the perimeter of the suspect's property. The LAV was loaded with team members and unit commanders, then deployed to evacuate the patrol officers. Under the protection of a team with ballistic shields and MP-5s, the patrol officers were safely loaded into the rear of the LAV via the ramp, while tactical team members assumed the perimeter positions. The LAV then drove to the front of the house to allow the unit commanders to recon the scene.

After negotiations proved fruitless, an assault plan was put into action. When the arrest team was in place, a diversion began at the rear of the house. The arrest team charged the front steps with their MP-5s. The suspect ran out the front door and was tackled by one of the officers from behind. It was later discovered that both of the family members in the house were already dead, though no shots had been fired from the time the local police had arrived on the scene.

The Westchester County SRT operates the only LAV-25 currently in the hands of a civilian police force. The eight-wheel unit can deploy a team of 12 officers and operate on land or as an amphibious craft. This particular vehicle was formerly leased to the FBI HRT and was on-scene at the Montana Freemen standoff in 1996.

5

CHAPTER FIVE

NYPD ESU

NYPD

The city of New York encompasses more than 320 square miles with a population over 7 million. The city consists of five boroughs: Manhattan, Brooklyn, Queens, the Bronx, and Staten Island. The New York City Police Department (NYPD) further divides these five boroughs into eight sub-boroughs with 76 precincts. In addition to Staten Island and the Bronx, Manhattan is divided into Manhattan North and Manhattan South. Likewise, Brooklyn is divided into Brooklyn North and Brooklyn South, and Queens is divided into Queens North and Queens South. Since 1993, crime in New York is down more than 44 percent and homicides are down more than 70 percent. In order to get an idea how big of a decrease is represented by 70 percent, there were more than 2,000 homicides in 1993, whereas 1998 had 629. According to recent FBI statistics, the city of New York is considered the safest large city in the United States.

The Water Tender will only see service in the event of civil unrest where the NYPD and FDNY deem the situation too dangerous for fire department personnel due to riot conditions.

One of the newer units in the ESU fleet sporting the new color scheme, the Jumper Response Vehicle carries large air bags that can be inflated to cushion the fall of a suicidal person who jumps from a building up to 10 stories tall. Equally important to its duties is the rigid hull boat, used for water rescues, that is carried on top of the truck's body. The crane is used to remove and replace the boat.

Three REPs and a CARV are in staging at a job in Manhattan.

The NYPD has over 38,000 uniformed, in addition to 9,000 civilian personnel, some of whom operate the cities many specialized vehicles. These vehicles are under the Special Operations Division (SOD), which includes the bomb squad, aviation, harbor, and the Emergency Services Unit (ESU). The ESU is separate from the precinct patrol divisions and operates under its own command structure.

The ESU consists of over 400 officers in the eight police patrol boroughs. The NYPD divides the city further into 10 different areas for ESU referred to simply as truck areas. Each truck area encompasses many precincts. In terms of vehicles, the unit consists of a "truck," patrol vehicles, and additional specialized units. A truck refers to a large rescue squad-type vehicle that has a walk-in body with interior and exterior storage. Every truck has its own separate quarters next to a precinct headquarters. The trucks are quartered inside and respond with other specialized units that are assigned to them. Additionally, for every truck, there are three to four Radio Emergency Patrol vehicles (REPs). Citywide, there are 10 trucks and 49 REPs. The REPs go by an alphabetical radio designation followed by the truck number that they run with. Depending on how many are assigned to a particular tour of duty, each REP will be referred to with a letter from *A* through *D*. For example, the first

Seven-Truck's rig has a conventional Navistar chassis with the same Saulsbury body as the other trucks. Every compartment is packed tightly with specialized equipment for any job that may come along.

REP on duty assigned to Ten-Truck is the "A or Adam car," known as A-10. If there is a second REP working the same area, it will be the "B or boy car" followed by the "C car," also known as the "Charlie Car." Both trucks and REPs run with two officers each.

As of this writing, the NYPD is taking delivery of a replacement fleet of trucks. The current fleet is mainly built on Ford C Series chassis with custom bodies by Saulsbury. The balance of the trucks have International, Mack, and Freightliner chassis. The newer units will all arrive with Mack chassis, Saulsbury bodies, and the updated NYPD paint scheme, which is an all white vehicle with blue stripes and markings.

Trucks

Trucks are outfitted to handle any situation that may occur. They are equipped for tactical police work including hostage scenarios and barricaded subjects, emotionally disturbed persons (EDPs), shootings, and warrant service. They are also equipped for building collapses, the rescue of people involved in accidents, aircraft emergencies, auto accidents with entrapment, suicidal subjects, animal complaints, hazardous material incidents, water rescues, and assisting with explosive ordnances (bombs).

From a tactical standpoint, they carry a small armory stocked with MP-5s, mini-14s, shotguns, Glocks, ballistic shields, battering rams, and each officer's tactical gear including vests, ballistic helmets, gas masks, and other personal items. If one of the officers assigned for a particular tour of duty is a trained sniper, then his rifle will be added to the arsenal carried onboard.

To handle rescue work, each truck has two hydraulic extrication tools with portable and truck-mounted generators, air bags, ropes, an electric generator, jacks, chains, a rabbit tool, an oxy-acetylene torch, a small jackhammer, an air chisel, drills, and several types of saws. They also have wood for shoring and blocking in addition to a special Caldo torch that will burn through metal or cement.

Diving gear for four divers, two ice-rescue suits, an inflatable three-person raft with an outboard motor and life vests are onboard for water rescues. Other gear includes Self-Contained Breathing Apparatus (SCBA) with spare bottles, a surface air rescue system with a tripod for confined space rescues, a 28-foot ground ladder, fire extinguishers, first aid supplies, and a defibrillator for medical emergencies. Still more equipment includes a stokes stretcher, a scoop stretcher, several portable hand lights, construction helmets, a port-a-power, and cord reels with

Two-Truck sits at a job in Manhattan. This unit features the more common Ford C-8000 Series cab-over design that is found on most of the ESU trucks. Some of the equipment that is carried is visible through the open compartment doors. Eight-Truck's Ford can be seen in the background.

100+ feet of electric cord to enable them to use tools and lights where there is no electrical source. Each truck is also equipped with a winch and a telescoping light tower that can extend above the vehicle and rotate 360 degrees to provide 2,000 watts of illumination.

REPs

Whereas the trucks are generally on standby in quarters waiting for an assignment, the workhorses of the ESU are the REPs. They are patrol vehicles built on Ford F350 pickup truck chassis with utility bodies that are customized to accommodate the equipment that they carry. At least one REP will be a first responder to motor vehicle accidents, tactical incidents, and rescue calls. They are equipped much like the trucks, though with less highly specialized equipment because of their size.

The rear compartment of every REP is set up for vehicle extrication with the "Jaws of Life" consisting of two Hurst hydraulic tools, generators, and accessories.

Officers from Eight-Truck check equipment before beginning their tour of duty in the Adam car, A-8.

Like the truck, a REP carries two hydraulic extrication tools with portable generators. Accessories include rams for supporting two objects to prevent a collapse, spreaders to pry crushed items apart, and cutters, which are a large scissors-like attachment used mainly for cutting the front posts of a car around the windshield so the roof can be taken off. They also have air bags, an assortment of hand tools, several saws, and the equipment necessary to jack up a public transit train car.

REPs also carry a stokes basket, a 16-foot ladder, SCBAs, and rope and rigging for rappelling and rescues. They have diving equipment that includes a dry suit with a full facemask, nec-essary in the poor conditions they encounter in many of the waterways. Each REP also has a push bumper to move vehicles out of traffic. All ESU officers are emergency medical technicians (EMTs), and first aid equipment and defibrillators are carried on the REPs.

Tactical equipment includes the officers' personal gear, shotgun, and now a semiautomatic rifle in response to the situation that occurred in Los Angeles (as outlined under Dearborn, MI). One aspect of the REP that is not part of a truck is the animal control kit. This includes a CO_2 pistol and rifle to subdue stray or dangerous animals. They also carry nooses to grab stray dogs.

Armored Vehicles

Officers taking fire will elicit the response of an armored vehicle. The ESU has three military surplus Peacekeeper armored personnel carriers. They are armored vehicles built around a modified Dodge pickup chassis and are spread throughout the city with different trucks. One is with Nine-Truck in Queens; another is with One-Truck in Manhattan South; and the third is with Three-Truck in the Bronx. Built to provide protection from small arms fire, these units can respond with lights and sirens directly to a scene.

For greater protection, or for the deployment of a tactical team in the face of larger arms fire, the ESU has three heavy armored personnel carriers. Resembling military tanks, these M75 military surplus units run on tracks, unlike the Peacekeepers, which drive on wheels. Referred to as Emergency Response Vehicles (ERVs), these units are quartered at Floyd Bennett Field. At least one of these units is always at a state of readiness on a lowboy trailer with a tractor hooked to it. It can be on the road in a matter of minutes responding to a scene that involves sniper fire or hostages. These units weigh in excess of 50,000 pounds. They are very quick and have surprisingly good maneuverability. An ERV can accommodate a crew of three and deploy a team of 8–12 tactical officers. There is a protected turret position at the top for the commander, two doors at the rear for quick deployment of an entry team, and lower positions for the driver and an assistant with an exterior hatch. One of the units is used for training purposes,

One of three ERVs that the NYPD ESU has at its disposal, this unit is kept in reserve status at Floyd Bennett Field for training. At least one ERV is on 24-hour standby on a flatbed trailer with an over-the-road tractor attached for immediate deployment.

The MALT runs out of Seven-Truck in Brooklyn next to the 75th Precinct. Built by Saulsbury on a Freightliner Business Class chassis, the MALT has two giant light towers capable of illuminating an area the size of a football stadium. Onboard generators can produce 200-amp electrical service, and with the help of hundreds of feet of electrical cable can supply power and lighting in the event of a power outage in the subway tunnels.

although it could go into service as a backup piece if the need arises.

Auxiliary Lighting

The NYPD has several units to supply outdoor lighting. The Mobile Auxiliary Lighting Truck (MALT) is assigned to Seven-Truck in Brooklyn. This is the largest of five light trucks.

Saulsbury built the unit on a Freightliner Business Class chassis. It has a 100-kW generator and the capacity to light an area as large as Grand Central Station. It has two telescoping light towers with a combined output of 9,000 watts. The MALT has 500- and 1,500-watt portable quartz lights, and can supply 50- and 100-amp service. It carries 200-amp, three-phase

Each compartment has steel-reinforced shelving that slides out for easy access to the cord reels, junction boxes, and other specialty equipment that is carried.

The generator truck is simply a box truck with an enormous generator capable of 90 kW of power. Combined with the MALT, these units can supply sufficient energy to power a 12-story building in the event of a power outage.

portable cord reels in addition to its 110/220-volt three-phase, 60-Hz generator. To keep everything running, the truck has three pump-fed diesel fuel tanks. The long cord reels are able to get power into the subways when it is needed from the truck at street level.

The other four mobile light units are Mobile Light Generators (MLGs) which have 7-kW generators and outlets to power 500-watt equipment. Each is built on a Ford F350 pickup truck and also has a telescoping light tower. These are assigned to One-, Three-, Six-, and Nine-Truck. Other available lighting equipment is in the form of 14 generators with conventional floodlights on telescoping masts. They have the capacity to produce 4 kWs, which is the average load of a single-family house. These have a trailer hitch that can be hooked up and pulled behind a REP.

Partially as a response to New York's famous blackout of 1977, ESU has generators as standard equipment on much of their fleet. One truck has a 90-kW generator to supplement all of the smaller generators, and to act as a tender for the MALT. The generator truck is a straight frame box truck on a 1980 International S1700 chassis with only 4,000 road miles on the odometer. Working together with the MALT, the two trucks can provide enough power to supply a 12-story building.

Other Specialized Vehicles

Eight-Truck in Brooklyn has three special pieces in addition to their truck and REPs. The first unit is one of two ESU Construction Accident Response Vehicles (CARV). This is a converted straight frame Grumman box truck with a lift gate on a Ford F600 Series medium-duty chassis. It responds to construction accident sites, building collapses, scaffold collapses, and trench rescues with equipment to stabilize a structure to rescue trapped victims. It is loaded with plywood, 4x4s, pneumatic saws, lights, a torch, a chop saw, support jacks, cord reels, air bags, and fans. Although some of these incidents will also bring a fire department response, the ESU would take precedence on any scene with known or suspected criminal acts involved. Except for the lights and siren, this looks like any

The interior of the CARV unit showing the lumber, metal jacks, cord reels, and other equipment that is used to shore up the site after construction accidents. This is one of two CARV trucks and lives with Eight-Truck in Brooklyn.

one of a number of conventional delivery trucks working in the city. The second CARV is with Three-Truck in the Bronx.

Eight-Truck also has a bomb squad support unit. They have one of the two TCVs in New York. It is built on a dual axle trailer to be hitched to a REP. The TCV is designed to transport explosive devices from an area where they would cause damage and injury to a remote area for disruption or intentional detonation. A TCV is designed to contain a blast completely within

ESU officers are returning lumber to the Eight-Truck's CARV after completing a job.

inside a building for loading. There is a ramp on the trailer, and the chamber will fit into an elevator if the capacity is sufficient. Weighing 4,000 pounds, the chamber sits on a manually operated lift device similar to those used in warehouses for moving heavy pallets. The second TCV is with Two-Truck in Manhattan North.

The bomb squad has two other special vehicles that are stationed at Floyd Bennett Field, both are tractor-drawn units. These two bomb carrier trucks are permanently attached to the trailers that carry them and are pulled by one of the International COE or Mack MR tractors. These unique trucks are called LaGuardia Trucks. Designed during the administration of Mayor LaGuardia in the 1940s, they are large vessels constructed of bridge cable. These shrapnel containment vessels are designed to withstand any potential blast from a device discovered in the city. As with the TCVs, a device will be loaded into one of the LaGuardia Trucks and transported with a police escort to a location away from the city.

Also quartered with Eight-Truck is a Jumper Response Vehicle. There are three of these units, all brand new. One is stationed with Four-Truck in the Bronx, and the third is with Six-Truck in Brooklyn South. Saulsbury built them on International 4700 LoProfile chassis with the T444E engine. They carry special air bags to catch people threatening to jump from buildings. The bags are rated for up to a 10-story building, and they also have at their disposal an air bag for a 20-story building. Two large fans are onboard to inflate the bags quickly. Like most of the ESU vehicles, the Jumper Response Vehicles are also equipped with a telescoping light tower. They carry extra cord reels for portable lights, first aid equipment, a hydraulic pump for special saws, a jackhammer, and pumping equipment. Extrication equipment is also part of the complement of tools on these trucks.

the chamber. There are quartz lights at all four corners of the trailer and a canvas tarp to conceal the chamber while also keeping it clean. Unlike some TCVs that are permanently attached to the trailer that carries them, these units can be removed from the trailer and taken

Eight-Truck's TCV is stored on a trailer. The chamber sits on a hand-operated forklift that will allow the entire vessel to be taken into a building and up an elevator that can support its weight. This serves to reduce the risk of transporting explosive devices through a building and down to the street.

One of the two LaGuardia trailers sits at Floyd Bennett Field for another assignment. The unique shrapnel containment vessel is built from bridge cable. It can withstand almost any blast that occurs within its chamber.

Water Rescue

The Jumper Response Vehicles also serve as water rescue/rescue support trucks. They have rafts as well as gear to equip four divers. On the roof of the truck's body is a rigid hull inflatable boat along with a 3,500-pound roof-mounted crane to remove and replace the boat.

ESU also has a Light Amphibious Re-Supply Craft (LARC). This odd-looking vehicle is capable of traveling on land using its wheels, or by sea with its outboard motor and propellers. The LARC is 14 feet wide and 14 feet tall with the ability to travel through the water and over sandbars, reaching six knots in the water. As with many of the other unique vehicles that ESU has, this is also a military surplus unit. It was originally used during the Vietnam War to offload equipment from ship to shore. The NYPD acquired this piece around 1992 to work in the shallow waters of Jamaica Bay. Its primary purpose is to serve as a rescue platform in the event of an airplane crash. It can be stationed in the middle of the bay to support divers for an extended rescue operation. In

Although the LARC doesn't see much action, it provides an important work platform for recovery operations that occur offshore.

addition to supporting divers, the LARC can serve as a launch for small boats and jet skis.

Another unit used to support water rescues is affectionately nicknamed the Baywatch Truck. This is a 1991 Chevy ex-military, double-wheeled pickup truck. Over the bed is a metal frame to support a rigid hull inflatable boat, a ladder, life preservers, and an outboard motor. It also carries a hydraulic extrication tool, diving gear, and ice-rescue suits. There is a trailer hitch to pull a Yamaha jet ski.

ESU also has a utility-type bucket truck that is built on a 1995 GMC Topkick chassis. It has body compartmentation similar to the electric and phone utility service trucks. Mounted to the frame is a 50-foot Aero-lift cherry picker with a bucket. This unit can assist at tactical situations by providing an elevated position to conduct reconnaissance or to assist a sniper in getting to an appropriate vantage point. There are other, non-tactical uses for this vehicle such as reaching stranded

The Baywatch truck is a quick response vehicle for water rescues. This unit responds from land whereas the harbor unit responds by water. The jet ski allows for a quick and highly maneuverable response with more agility than a rigid hull watercraft.

The NYPD ESU hazardous materials support vehicle is stationed at Floyd Bennett Field. This unit responds to any haz mat incident, bringing spare air cylinders and SCBA setups in addition to scene lighting and a 55-gallon drum for the storage and disposal of hazardous product.

victims or providing a position to monitor crowds at major events in the city.

Haz Mat

Along with the fire department (FDNY), ESU also handles hazardous materials incidents (haz mat). Support vehicles for haz mat operations are based at the Floyd Bennett Field. One unit is built on a 1990 Chevy chassis with a Utilimaster body. Saulsbury customized the truck's interior to carry air bottles, SCBAs, containers for hazardous products, and various support equipment. The other haz mat vehicle is the haz mat decon trailer. The unit consists of one of the ESU tractors and a 40-foot trailer for decontaminating people exposed to hazardous materials. There are two boilers onboard to supply hot water for 16 showers. It also has showers that will accommodate patients on a stretcher. One side of the trailer has two panels that span the

The Hazardous Materials Decontamination Unit is equipped to provide "clean" and "dirty" showers for officers or civilians who are exposed to dangerous chemicals.

entire length of the truck. These panels are hinged and can be supported by poles to form the roof for two changing rooms alongside the truck. Canvas panels unroll to the ground for privacy. These two external rooms allow for clean (decontaminated) and dirty (contaminated) changing rooms.

One special unit that has not seen action in quite some time is a converted military surplus water pumper for fighting fires. Based at Floyd Bennett Field, this unit would be called into service for crowd control or for a fire during a hostile situation that would prevent a response from the FDNY. It is built on a 6x6 International chas-

sis and carries large diameter hard suction hose for drafting water, fire extinguishers, and several thousand feet of conventional fire hose. It also has a truck-mounted turret for discharging large volumes of water.

Other special SOD units include mobile command and communications vehicles, bomb squad vehicles and robots, and the canine units. The aviation division has two Bell Model 412 helicopters, a Long Ranger, and a Jet Ranger. The marine division and the harbor unit have five vessels between 48 and 55 feet long, two 36-foot vessels, and four 30-foot vessels.

INDEX